Praise for *Secrets of Property...*

"It's always EASIER, CHEAPER and FAS[TER] ... successfully achieved what you'd like to do. This book is invaluable ... if you have an interest in real estate because it allows you to consider and evaluate which approach to property wealth might best suit you."

Hans Jakobi – Australia's Wealth Coach®
Professional Investor, International Best-Selling Author, Educator

"This book is a must-read for anybody who is serious about investing. It gives you a snapshot into the lives of the people who've made it and teaches you many new strategies to realise your dream even sooner."

Liliane Harb – Aspiring Real Estate Investor

"As a financial planner, I'm always advising my clients to educate themselves about the various facets of asset protection, investing and creating wealth. This book is one of the most comprehensive guides to property I've seen. Highly recommended!"

Randall Yip – Senior Financial Planner, Phillips Dean Brickwood

"I'm just starting out in property. This book has given me an excellent opportunity to achieve my goals, without having to make the major mistakes that the property greats have before me."

Spencer Ferreira – A Really Good-Looking Business Student

"In my industry I see so many people with all the technical information about property investing, yet who never seem to take any action. This book gives you the motivational spark needed to get moving. A great read!"

Mike Small – Finance Broker, X Inc.

"After reading *Secrets of Property Millionaires Exposed* it becomes very clear how simple and easy property investing is and the importance of understanding which investment strategy is best for you."

Andrew Melhem – Architect and Property Investor

"With a wife and two kids to provide for, I want to make good financial decisions. Great to see a book that asks the questions you have always wanted to ask a millionaire. Inspirational!"

Simon DeGaris – Property Valuer

"This was an absolutely amazing book and a valuable tool for anyone else looking to get involved in property investing. It's easy to read and outlines the practical steps of what to do. But best of all, the information is from people that have already done it and now have great wealth."

Elizabeth Goodman – Business Owner and Property Investor

"My wife and I started investing in property some time ago with just one property. But last year we branched out to where we now own four properties. These were purchased as positive cash flow properties to supplement our superannuation in our retirement. This book gave us some great ideas to go on to greater heights."

Dr. John Millar – Property Investor

"As a town planner, I've been associated with property development for over 40 years. This book succeeds in demystifying the principles of development and investing, by bringing to us the basic lessons learnt from experienced, down-to-earth practitioners. Well done."

Max Fragar – National Councillor, Planning Institute Australia

SECRETS OF PROPERTY MILLIONAIRES EXPOSED!

Featuring written material by ★ John Fitzgerald ★ Hans Jakobi
★ Dymphna Boholt ★ Ed Chan ★ Craig Turnbull ★ and more

DALE BEAUMONT
& COLIN B. FRAGAR WITH FOREWORD BY SIMON BAKER

Disclaimer
All the information, techniques, skills and concepts contained within this publication are of the nature of general comment only, and are not in any way recommended as individual advice. The intent is to offer a variety of information to provide a wider range of choices now and in the future, recognising that we all have widely diverse circumstances and viewpoints. Should any reader choose to make use of the information contained herein, this is their decision, and the contributors (and their companies), authors and publishers do not assume any responsibilities whatsoever under any conditions or circumstances. It is recommended that the reader obtain their own independent advice.

FIRST EDITION 2005
Copyright © 2005 Dream Express International Pty Ltd
All rights reserved. No part of this publication may be reproduced, stored in a retrieval system, or transmitted in any form or by any means, electronic, mechanical, photocopying, recording or otherwise, without the prior written permission from the publisher.

Beaumont, Dale   Fragar, Colin B.
Secrets of Property Millionaires Exposed

ISBN 0-9757974-2-5
National Library of Australia Cataloguing-in-Publication entry:

1. Real Estate Investment   2. Interviews – Australia   3. Beaumont, Dale   I. Title

Published by Dream Express Publishing
A division of Dream Express International Pty Ltd
PO Box 567, Crows Nest, NSW 1585 Australia
Email: info@SecretsExposed.com.au
Website: www.SecretsExposed.com.au

Distributed in Australia by Gary Allen
For further information about orders:
Phone: +61 2 9725 2933
Email: customerservice@garyallen.com.au

Editing by Simone Tregeagle [simone@inkcommunications.com.au]
Layout and typesetting by Bookhouse [www.bookhouse.com.au]
Cover design by Jay Beaumont [www.thecreativehouse.com]
Illustrations by Grant Tulloch [info@secretsexposed.com.au]
Printed and bound by McPherson's Printing Group
[www.mcphersonsprinting.com.au]

To my amazing and super-talented love bunny, Katherine. Your continued belief inspires me every day.

Dale Beaumont

To the best parents I could ever ask for. Thankyou for your continued love, support and wisdom.

Colin B. Fragar

Acknowledgments

As with any major project there are a number of very special people who contributed to making it happen, and we'd like to take a short moment to say 'Thank You'.

First, to the people who said NO to us when they were asked to be part of this book; it really helped to provide extra motivation and made us even more determined to see it through. A special acknowledgement to Neil Jenman for your supportive, yet honest letter.

To each of our parents, Paul and Chrissy Beaumont and Max and Wendy Fragar, for all of your support and home-cooked meals over the many, many days of editing.

To Jay (Dale's brother), thanks for designing the covers for all of our books (including those we haven't even started). One day we are going to pay you back – with interest of course! Also to Simone (from Ink Communications) our wonderful editor; thanks for seeing the vision right from the start and for all your late nights to ensure that it all got done.

Now to our very generous friends, who either helped formulating the hundreds of different questions for the book, or took the time to read 66,951 words and tell us what they thought. These wonderful people are: Leticia Ferreira, Brent Williams, Ryan Butler, Fiona Anson, John and Liliane Harb, Andrew Melham, Chi Nguyen, Stuart Zadel, Katie Hensley, Simon DeGaris, John Millar and Spencer Ferreira. To coin a not-so-original phrase: we love you all!

And finally to the wonderful people who thankfully said YES! It certainly was a big thrill and a whole lot of fun working with each of you. Even though one or two of you were a little difficult to track down at times (we won't mention any names), we did eventually get all the material and it was certainly worth the wait. Also to the people that we have been able to meet personally (you know who you are), thanks for the opportunity and we look forward to continuing the friendship.

CONTENTS

PREFACE		1
FOREWORD		7
INTRODUCTION		9
CRAIG TURNBULL	SEE THE POSSIBILITY	11
PATRICK BRIGHT	A SENSE OF URGENCY	29
DYMPHNA BOHOLT	CREATING THE CASH COW	49
JOHN FITZGERALD	MILLIONAIRE IN A YEAR	65
GORDON GREEN	INCOME VERSUS GROWTH	85
HANS JAKOBI	INTANGIBLE REWARDS	105
RICK OTTON	THAT'S A WRAP	129
SAM VANNUTINI	RENOVATE FOR PROFIT	147
ED CHAN	TAX MATTERS	165
GARY & JENNY LEATHER	THE POWER OF THE PAIR	183
PETER COMBEN	RISKY BUSINESS	201
FINAL THOUGHTS		221

PREFACE

If I were in your position right now I'd be wondering if I really needed to read this section. However, if I could ask you to resist the temptation to skip ahead for just a few minutes, I'd like to share with you a few of the reasons why this book has been created and how you can use it to impact your life.

When I was growing up I heard somewhere that there are two ways to live your life: the first is through 'trial and error' and the second is through 'other people's experience'. At the time I dismissed it as just another one of those sayings that sounds good, but doesn't make much sense. Then, like most teenagers I finished school with stars in my eyes thinking, 'This is great! My education is over – no more books, no more lectures, no more people telling me what to do'. How wrong I was. After a few months of bouncing around, not quite sure of what to do next, I stumbled across the idea of personal development and started to hear concepts such as:

- Formal education will earn you a living, but self-education will make you a fortune.
- Work harder on yourself that you do on your job.
- You will be the same person five years from now, except for the people you meet and the books you read.
- Don't wish that your job were easier, wish that you were better.
- You are your own greatest asset, so you must invest in yourself.

Since November 2000, I have been totally committed to becoming my own most valuable asset. After attending hundreds of seminars, listening to thousands of hours of CDs and reading shelves of books, I have discovered that the people who truly succeed aren't any smarter, better looking or harder working than anyone else – they just think differently and have learnt to incorporate different values into their lives.

I am now in the very fortunate position of being able to travel internationally to present personal development seminars to teenagers and I am often asked, 'What is the one thing you need to know to be successful?' My answer is always the same: 'The one thing that you need to know is that there is not *one* thing that you need to know to be successful'. I've learnt that success is multifaceted and that mastering one principle of success or area of your life isn't going to take you to the top – the more you master, the more successful you will become. But if I *did* have to identify one of the most important success strategies, it would be this: *'Find out what successful people do and do the same thing until you get the same results'*.

That's what this book is all about. The only difference is, instead of you going out and finding successful people, we've brought them to you.

You see, whatever you want in life, whatever you are shooting for, chances are that someone else is already living it. They have already invested years of their life and probably hundreds of thousands of dollars, they've made lots of mistakes, learnt from them and eventually succeeded. So why would you want to waste your own time, money and effort through 'trial and error' when you can fast-track your success by learning from 'someone else's experience'? As Sir Isaac Newton said, 'If I have seen further it is because I have been standing on the shoulders of giants'.

Every time you pick up a book, attend a seminar or interview a successful person, you are compressing years of life experience into a few hours. With any of the 'Secrets Exposed' books, you can multiply that by between twelve and sixteen people and you're looking at around 250+ years of experience and wisdom ready and waiting for you. It won't prevent you from making mistakes of your own, far from it, but it will help you to make more calculated and purposeful decisions, rather than big, misguided and ignorant ones.

There is no shortage of information about how to achieve proficiency or even greatness in any area of life these days. Go to any bookstore or library and you'll find the shelves sagging with titles from experts, all with their own theories and ways of doing things. But what I have discovered is lacking in almost all of these books is INSPIRATION. What's missing is role models and mentors – the stories of people we can all look up to. People who started out exactly like you – with a dream in their hearts and with all the same fears and insecurities. Given the choice between reading a textbook or a dozen success stories about people who have actually done something, I'd take the success stories any day of the week. I'm not saying that theoretical information isn't important, of course it is, but having presented hundreds of talks to all different types of audiences, I can confidently say that it's always the stories that move people. It's the whole, "If he or she did it, then so can I" that gets inside people's hearts. When we're inspired we get motivated and then we take positive action which leads to results.

The 'Secrets Exposed' books are not intended to be a one-stop-shop. They are an introduction to the wealth of knowledge available to you and to some of the real success stories of people who have reached the top in their chosen field of endeavour. That's why at the back of each book you will find most of the contributors' contact details and some of their other products and services that are available to help you continue your journey.

So, how did the whole idea for the 'Secrets Exposed' books come about?

Well, in 1998, when I was around seventeen, my nan gave me a copy of a book titled *Collective Wisdom*, by Brett Kelly. In it were transcripts of face-to-face interviews with a whole lot of prominent Australian personalities. And it was a fantastic read. Since then I have seen a handful of random 'success story' books, but the challenge I find with most of them is that they are either transcripts of interviews, that never really make complete sense in the printed form, or they are written by writers who paraphrase someone else's story. The result tends to be a diluted message that doesn't really allow you to get a sense of the individual's personality or character.

In around 2001 I read my first *Chicken Soup for the Soul* book and realised that there were dozens and dozens of related titles designed to meet the needs of different people's areas of interest. I thought that was pretty neat.

It wasn't until January 2004 that the 'Secrets Exposed' idea boiled over. I was in my hotel room in Singapore relaxing after six straight days of presenting to hundreds of teenagers. I was reflecting on the ideas that had been shared with them. One of the most important was to seek out those who have already achieved what you want and ask them lots of questions. I was plagued by the thought that only a small percentage would act on that very valuable advice and that most would never take the step due to a lack of confidence, fear of rejection or an inability to contact the people they needed.

That's when it hit me…'What if I could find the people and put together a number of books covering a range of different areas?' I knew it would take a lot of effort, so for the next three days, I sat in my hotel room and developed the basis of an entire system to make it happen.

Based on my experience with other books, I decided that these books had to be non-time specific and be written (not spoken) by the people themselves. This way the answers would be planned and well thought-out, providing richer content and more interesting reading. I also wanted to make sure that there was an even balance between practical 'how to' information and inspirational stories that gave an insight into the highs and lows of people's real journeys. I also wanted to ensure that a percentage of every book sold was donated to a charity relating to the nature of that particular book.

When I arrived home I got into action. However, between working out of a tiny one-bedroom flat and trying to manage two other demanding businesses, my plans were a little slow in the beginning and I had to be resourceful. So I bought a plastic tub and turned the boot of my car into a mobile office! Anytime I could find a spare hour or two, I'd park myself at the gym or a nearby coffee shop and make calls from my mobile phone.

Putting these books together has been both time-consuming and demanding, but it has also been a real privilege for me to have the opportunity to work with each of the people involved in the various books. Thank you, to each of you, for making it possible!

Well, I think you've heard enough from me. Now it's time for you to discover for yourself the wonderful wisdom contained in these pages. I hope that you enjoy the read as much as we've enjoyed putting it together. And who knows, maybe one day we will be reading your story?

Dream Big!

Dale Beaumont
Creator of 'Secrets Exposed' Series
Sydney, Australia

FOREWORD

In any undertaking, no matter how large or small, success is often attributed to three key areas: a great strategy, a strong focus on execution and a manic passion to make it happen. It doesn't matter whether you are multi-million dollar company or a property investor – identifying a great strategy and executing it with passion is what gives you the greatest chance of success.

A well thought-out strategy provides a clear direction. It should articulate what the objectives are, what resources it requires and how much value it can create. Side-by-side with strategy is execution. Successful undertaking focus on ensuring that they apply the right resources, that they constantly measure progress and are not distracted. And the 'x- factor' that ties it all together is passion. Sometimes even a mediocre strategy and sub-optimal execution can be overcome by the sheer passion to make it happen.

At realestate.com.au, we have followed this simple approach. In 2001 we put in place a simple growth strategy and then focused our entire team on its execution. We had a single-minded commitment to the achievement of our plan and we made sure that we invested the right level of resources to make it happen. The result is that over the past four years we have turned a business with a market capitalisation of $8 million into one with a market capitalisation of $180 million. We have increased our revenues eight-fold and have become profitable.

In this book you will find many more examples of successful property investors who have taken this same approach. Each has spent time developing the specific property investment strategies, and each has then passionately focused their efforts on execution, with some amazing results.

The authors, Dale and Colin, have created this book using the same methodology – they established a clear vision and passionately executed that vision in the development of a book that is full of tips and techniques for any property investor.

I hope that this book helps you to create your own property investment vision and that the stories and experiences of those who have tread the path before you encourage you to passionately follow that vision through to becoming a property investment millionaire yourself.

Simon Baker
Chief Executive Officer
realestate.com.au Ltd

INTRODUCTION

Now, more than ever before, people want to create wealth. Not just a few extra dollars each month, but enough to provide the genuine financial freedom to live the life and lifestyle they truly desire. For the last few decades there has been a raging debate on the best method, strategy or approach to achieve this freedom, and in many ways it's property investing that is at the forefront of this debate. Go to any bookshop and you'll find the shelves sagging with hundreds of wealth creation books, the majority of which are about property.

Over recent years the flood of information has brought with it a new wave of high-gloss marketeers and property spruikers, leaving people more confused and overwhelmed than ever. That's the reason why we decided to write this book. In the beginning our plan was very simple, *'Find the most successful people in property we can, ask them how they did it, and put it in a format that would be accessible to anyone'*.

More specifically, the criteria for the people we were looking for was that they needed to have built the majority of their portfolio in Australia, have a net worth of more than $1 million, and represent good values and ethics. We also wanted the people who contributed to not just be talkers but doers. In other words, we wanted people who were actively investing in today's market.

So after eighteen months of endless phone calls, emails and editing, some of the most valuable and exciting information ever gathered is ready to be absorbed. However, before you go diving into it there are a few other important points we'd like to mention.

First, this is like no other book in that you aren't going to be reading about one person's strategy or approach. You are going to be reading all of them: positive cash flow, negative gearing, renovations, joint ventures, subdivision, property development and vendor financing, to name just a few. Each of the contributors will present their path and reason for pursuing it, empowering you with the information you need to develop your own personal goals and game plan.

Second, there is something for everyone in this book. Whether you are a sophisticated investor looking for a new edge, or an aspiring investor looking to get started, you'll find dozens, if not hundreds of great ideas. Our recommendation is that you read this book once right through, then re-read it again marking all of your favourite points with a highlighter pen.

Third, please know that this book is by no means a one-stop-shop. Once you have defined your goals and developed your approach, we would encourage you to seek more information, that's why at the back of the book we have included the websites of each contributor. You'll find that many of them have their own books, CD programs or live seminars so you can continue to expand your knowledge.

Fourth, as you flick through the book, you'll find that some of the contributors have generously offered valuable gifts to all of our readers. All you need to do is visit our website, follow the instructions and you'll be able to download every one of those gifts, absolutely free.

And finally, remember it's what you do *after you read this book* that is going to determine its real value. So get out there, apply what you've learnt, and please when you reach a goal, no matter how big or small, email us so we can read *your* success story!

Enjoy!

Dale Beaumont and Colin B. Fragar

Email: info@SecretsExposed.com.au

SEE THE POSSIBILITY

Craig Turnbull

CRAIG TURNBULL

> " Buy the best quality property, in the best location you can reasonably afford and never, ever sell it. "

PROFILE

CRAIG TURNBULL

Craig Turnbull was born in Fremantle, Western Australia, in 1963. As one of four children in a family that struggled to make ends meet, he learnt the value of money early in life and grew up with a keen desire to become wealthy. In 1982, he read the first BRW Rich 200 List and discovered that most of Australia's wealthiest people either made or held their wealth in property. He began his real estate investment career at the age of nineteen and was a millionaire by the age of 28.

Craig had many early successes in property investment, followed by several setbacks. But rather than treat these as negative events, he re-adjusted his approach and turned them into the learning opportunities that have led him to become known as a 'property guru'. Craig discovered that he had a talent for sharing his property investment experiences, and in 2001 began his education company Property Millionaire Pty Ltd. Since then, he has taught thousands of people how to create wealth through real estate. Over the years the company has expanded into a boutique financial services group offering mentoring programs, finance broking and property-search services – it is now known as Aspire International.

Craig is the author of three national best-selling property investment books: *It's Easy to Invest in Property*, *It's Easy to be a Property Millionaire* and *Unlimited Cashflow – It's Easy to Make Money in Property*. He is also an international keynote speaker on property investment and success motivation.

Craig lives in Perth with his partner and shares his weekends with his two sons. When he is not working, you'll find him looking at property, at the beach or indulging his passion for travel.

Why did you decide to start investing in property?

I come from a family of four children and even though both of my parents worked very hard, it always seemed to me that money was a struggle; my desire to be rich stemmed from this. In 1982, when I was in my late teens, I read the first ever BRW Rich List and realised that most of the people on the list had either built their fortune or held the majority of their wealth in property – so I reasoned, if it was good enough for the richest people in the country, then why not me?

What do you love about property?

Property is one of my passions. It's something that most people are comfortable with and to own your own home is the 'Great Australian Dream'. Property is solid; it's real and you can drive past it – every day if you want to!

Historically, property has steadily increased in value. It doesn't increase every year, as we know it moves in cycles, but over time it always moves upward. Another great thing is that it produces a steady weekly income that grows each year. It is relatively stable and probably the lowest risk of all investments – just ask the banks which asset class they will lend the most money against! Anyone can own it and you don't have to be ultra-rich.

It's also easy to add value to your property to increase wealth, which is a major advantage over share ownership. I'll give you an example: given a roller and a big tin of paint, do you think you could add value to your ANZ shares by going on down to their head office and giving it a fresh coat of paint? Probably not! Yet, apply the same coat of paint to a property you have just bought and chances are that your equity will increase because you have increased the desirability of the home and therefore its value. I have never known a property to drop in value by half or even to nothing overnight, as can be the case with the share market. Even if the

> **To become wealthy through property, you must have a belief and a positive expectation that you can achieve your goal.**

building were to be destroyed, it could always be rebuilt through insurance, and even if you are uninsured, there is always the land which has a residual value.

In my opinion, property, when carefully selected, financed and managed is the best investment that the average person can make.

What was your very first investment property and what did you have to do to get it?

I bought my very first investment property when I was nineteen. It was an old home that had been divided into four small bed-sitter units. It was priced at $65,000 and was in an area that had great long-term potential for capital growth. What attracted me most were the four lots of rent. At the time I was working in a mining town, so I asked my parents to have a look at the property for me. It turned out that it was at the back of a large block and four more units had been built at the front of the block. My folks liked the look of the property so I bought it, sight unseen, and my parents bought the four units at the front for around $30,000 each. It proved to be a fantastic investment; recently the whole property was sold for $750,000 after being owned by my family for around twenty years.

I struggled with the bank to buy the property. I was only nineteen years old, I had only been in my job for three months and I'd never used credit before. On top of that, I only had $4,000 saved and the bank wanted a 10% deposit, plus costs, which meant I needed $8,000. For several days I was scared that my fledgling property career was over, until I started thinking outside the square; I borrowed the $4,000 as a personal loan from another bank and went back to the first bank and got my loan approved.

What is the single most important lesson you've learnt about property investing?

Throughout my investing career I have experimented with all kinds of crazy and interesting ways to make money from property and I've managed to do as many things right as I have done wrong! There was no one offering the types of books, courses and education that are available today when I started out – I did it the hard way. Over time, I realised that it really could be much simpler and I developed a rule, my 'Golden Rule for Property': *buy the best quality property, in the best location you can reasonably afford and never, ever sell it.* It's a simple enough statement in itself, but rules don't make you rich.

To become wealthy through property (or any other type of investing for that matter), you must have a belief and a positive expectation that you can achieve your goal. Any kind of success begins with a belief in what it is that you can achieve, followed by an unshakeable commitment and a plan of action to carry out your belief.

What advice would you give to someone who wants to get started in property investing?

It's so easy to go out and buy property. Really! Yet so many people fail to make any preparations or plans for what they want to achieve. They just open up the newspaper on a Saturday morning, wave their finger over the suburb they want to live in, bang it down onto the page and go out and buy the property that their finger landed on. Sadly, this approach is more the norm than the exception.

The first thing you must do as a new property investor is make a plan. This should include details such as whether you are planning to invest for capital growth or income, whether you will be buying new or old houses or units, and whether you will be using short-term strategies like renovating or flipping, or if you are happier just operating on a buy-and-hold basis.

> "...when I realised that *I* was responsible for everything that happened, my income and wealth grew proportionately."

The easiest way to create your plan is to first clearly envisage your ultimate outcome and the time period within which you plan to achieve it. For example, your goal might be to become a property millionaire within ten years. Then, work backwards to where you are today, filling in the steps along the way that will get you to your outcome.

The bottom line is, don't start investing without a plan!

What were some of the challenges you had to overcome on the journey to achieving your financial goals?

I've had so many! At times it seemed to me that the universe was constantly coming up with things to test how badly I really wanted to succeed and be wealthy. When I first started, I was constantly told, 'you're too young', or, 'no, I am not submitting that low offer', or, 'sorry, we can't lend you any more money'. Coming up with the monthly repayments, especially when rates were due and at tax time, was very difficult for me. In the early days I knew very little about how to manage my cash flow and I hadn't yet realised that property could actually provide you with an income in some circumstances. I just bought everything I could hoping it would go up in value.

By far the biggest challenge was overcoming my own beliefs about what I could achieve. My self-worth was constantly telling me that all of this investing stuff was a bit unreal and besides, who was I to think that I could get rich? Once I learnt that becoming wealthy was really possible, and more importantly, understood that it was possible for *me*, I began to grow as a person. And when I realised that *I* was responsible for everything that happened, my income and wealth grew proportionately.

If you had to start again with nothing, what would you do?

I have a great answer for this one because I really *did* have to start again with nothing. After I lost my money I spent a lot of time trying to figure out what went wrong. I realised that what had happened was entirely due to two of the most powerful motivators in the world: fear and greed. I spent a couple of years blaming everyone else for what had happened to me, but the day I accepted responsibility for my actions was the day that my life changed for the better.

The next step was deciding where it was I wanted to go from there; in other words, what my outcome would be. I set new goals so I had something to aim for; these were my 'whys', my reasons for getting up early and staying up late. I re-evaluated my strategy and made a new plan, which included getting some extra education in business and real estate. Part of my plan was to implement some property strategies that did not require a lot of money, since I didn't have any. They included the 'flip', which is a 'buy low and sell high quickly' technique that can generate fast cash and I planned to use the profit generated to fund renovation projects, which have the capacity to add value quickly. I also planned to use my research skills to put together great renovation and development deals, for which I could bring in other investors with capital. To balance things out, I put decent deposits on long-term 'buy-and-hold' deals so that my cash flow would be neutral at worst. The last thing I did was commit to taking persistent and constant action toward the achievement of my goals.

You are well-acquainted with just about every property investment strategy, is any one really better than another?

There are so many ways to make money from real estate, such as renovating, flipping, developing, positive cash flow, negative gearing, and buy-and-hold, to name just a few. And there are just as many people out there telling you that the way they favour investing in property is the only way to go. That concerns me because what they are really saying is that everyone is the same in their financial goals, knowledge, income, age, time availability, cash, equity and so on. But if you have no cash and no borrowing capacity, how can a negative gearing strategy work for you? If you have a high income with plenty of cash and not much time, then a long-term buy-and-hold strategy with negative gearing might suit you. People who have a lot of time commitments may be at a disadvantage in time-intensive strategies like renovating. And people who want to get into property development need a lot of knowledge, planning and research skills.

Each strategy has its own strengths and weaknesses. It is imperative that you choose one, or possibly two strategies that you can become very, very good at and make your wealth grow that way. I found that trying to use too many strategies split my focus and I ended up causing myself some grief.

What is 'flipping' and what does it involve?

The 'flip' is a fun little strategy that anyone can use to make money in real estate. It's fun because you don't need any money, you don't (necessarily) have to qualify for a bank loan and it can generate lots of cash very quickly. Interested? I thought so…read on.

The essence of a flip is remarkably simple: buy low and sell high, quickly. Translating this into real estate language, you must buy property well under market value and resell it quickly at a slight discount to what is on offer in the open market. It's not rocket science but the reason it's not done more often is because people don't think it can be done. People think that surely no one will sell a property for less than it is worth – which is absolutely and totally incorrect. Vendors sell below value every day as their circumstances change due to marriage, birth, death, illness, job loss or transfer. To find suitable properties to flip, you must ask, and you must make lots and lots of offers. To find the prince, you must kiss a lot of frogs, right? Be prepared to submit lots of offers before one gets accepted. This takes a determined effort, a lot of discipline and a very thick skin.

What makes a flip work is having a buyer ready to take the property from you before you actually buy it. With the correct set up, theoretically, you can own the property for just a few minutes before your pre-arranged buyer purchases it from you. All you get is one big, fat cheque!

Do you recommend new or old property?

Each has its benefits and drawbacks. Which is better comes down to what's most appropriate based on your preferred property investment strategy.

To summarise the main points: new property is probably more appealing to tenants, it will have higher rental returns, higher depreciation benefits, lower maintenance costs and it will be years before it suffers from economic obsolescence. On the flip side, it will usually cost you more than old property, you can't add value to it by renovating (it's new) and it is unlikely that you'll be able to negotiate much off the price. Old property is mostly cheaper, often located in established areas close to amenities, and value can be added quickly. On the downside are higher maintenance costs which means lower cash flow, lower depreciation benefits, usually lower rents and out-dated design.

What are some of the techniques that real estate agents use to persuade inexperienced buyers?

There are so many techniques used to persuade people to buy. As a licensed real estate agent myself, and having had around twenty years' experience, I have had the benefit of numerous sales training programs and have learnt techniques from the best (and worst) salespeople.

A clever agent will line up the properties he or she wants to show in a specific order. The first will be terrible, the second a bit

> ❝ I found that trying to use too many strategies split my focus and I ended up causing myself some grief. ❞

better and the third just right. If the buyer shows any interest, the first thing agents are taught to do is prey on the purchaser's fear of missing out by saying something like, 'There is another buyer'. Usually, this is enough to panic most people into doing something. If not, there are other sales closes such as the 'Benjamin Franklin', where the agent helps the buyer to list the positives of the property and then keeps quiet while the purchaser struggles to find the negatives after having thought of all the good things first. Another good one is when the buyer asks if something they see is included, such as a dishwasher. The agent writes it down on the offer and says something like, 'Let's see if we can get it for you'. I have lost count of the number of dishwashers that have been sold with houses attached!

The smartest thing you can do as a buyer is to be aware of the agents' techniques and understand that they are just doing what they are trained to do – that is to help you make a decision, you just need to be sure that it's the right one for you.

What are some of your favourite negotiation techniques when buying property?

I have used a lot of different techniques throughout my investment career. The most common is the 'low-ball', which is low price, high deposit, short settlement. This is used when there is a hint of time-pressure on the vendor. The 'first and final' is just like the low-ball except that you short-circuit the back-and-forth negotiation process by making one take-it or leave-it offer. The 'full price' is used when you are sure that the property is underpriced or that you can get some creative terms, such as a long settlement period. Finally, there is the 'over-price' offer. Use this one with caution, as it is only successful when you can add value really quickly and if the vendor will offer you some vendor finance that will allow you flexibility on repayments.

The key to negotiating successfully is understanding your vendor's situation so that you can design an offer with a win-win outcome. What would the point be in offering full price on a property with a twelve-month settlement if the bank is coming next week to take the property back?

What is the scariest thing that has happened to you in your property career?

In hindsight, this story is probably one of the funniest from early in my career, although it was more of a fright at the time!

I was driving past a property on a busy road leading into the city, when I noticed a 'For Sale' sign at the front which was leaning over and about to fall onto the dirt. My bargain radar began to beep so I turned the corner and circled back, pulling up into the driveway. Right away I could see that the property needed work and clearly no money had been spent on it recently. I purchased it for $46,000, down from the original asking price of $59,000. I didn't bother with an internal inspection and although I knew there were tenants, I had not met them.

After I settled on the property, I arrived planning to introduce myself to the tenant – the person who was going to help me pay for my new house. I knocked on the door and was greeted with a growling, 'Jus' a minute', followed by some loud banging and hammering. A short while later the door swung open and standing before me was the biggest man I had ever seen; he was wearing a leather vest, had tattooed arms the size of tree trunks, smelled like three-month-old tuna and held a can of beer in one hand and a greasy spanner in the other.

My tenant, the bikie, had just finished stripping his Harley Davidson in my lounge room. It was at this point in my investment career that I made the decision to always employ a professional property manager rather than handle the management myself!

> **❝ I have lost count of the number of dishwashers that have been sold with houses attached! ❞**

What do you think are the most common mistakes that new investors make?

There's a section in my book, *It's Easy to be a Property Millionaire*, called '10 Most Common Mistakes'. Some of them are: lack of a plan, not enough research, being emotional instead of analytical, being impatient, inappropriate financing and choosing the wrong property.

Another mistake that many new investors make, which most affects their ability to keep on their investment path, is paying too much for their first property. Not buying at a discount means you miss out on instant equity and as a result you either have to wait around for the property to increase in value or you have to renovate quickly in order to add value.

If anyone can succeed in property no matter what their current financial circumstances are, what do you think holds people back from becoming property millionaires?

In a word, *belief.*

I've written three books on property investing: *It's Easy to Invest in Property*, which is an introduction; *It's Easy to be a Property Millionaire*, which is a national best-seller; and a more advanced book that was originally titled *It's Easy to be a Property Multi-Millionaire.* This book sold well, but not nearly as well as the 'Millionaire' book, despite it containing far more powerful information and enough knowledge to enable a person to work for themselves as a full-time property investor. After doing some market research, I discovered that people weren't buying it because the title scared them; they just could not believe that they could ever become multi-millionaires. The 'Millionaire' book suffers a little from this too.

People look at where they are today and project forward in one huge jump to what, for many, is the ultimate target – millionaire status. But for most people, that jump looks too huge, so they don't start the journey. They remain in their own comfort zone, which will see them living on a pension or in relative poverty later in life.

Interestingly, we changed the name of the multi-millionaire book to *Unlimited Casfflow – It's Easy to Make Money in Property* – and guess what? Sales took off, even though the book was otherwise unchanged. Perception is reality.

What do you say to people who think it is too late for them to get into the market?

It's never too late. I often speak to people at seminars and on the radio who think at age 55 they are on the downward slope and way too old. That's just not true. People are living so much longer these days and we

> **You cannot deal with any kind of fear by running from it, ignoring it or trying to rationalise it away. You must confront it head-on.**

will need assets that grow in value and income to look after us when we stop working, so why not make a start?

Legend has it that Colonel Sanders started KFC when he was 65 years old, right after getting his first pension cheque and deciding that it just wasn't enough. His determination and desire for more changed the eating habits of the world and made him a wealthy man. What if he had given up, or not started, just because someone told him he was too old?

The other thing people say to me about missing out is when property has been going up and they think that the moment they buy it will go down. So they wait for prices to drop before they step up and commit to owning property. This really comes down to a basic fear. Even if you do pay top dollar for a property at the peak of the market and it comes down in price, historically, over time, prices come back and exceed their previous highs. Property can be very forgiving over time.

What common fears do people have about property investing, and how can you overcome them?

Without doubt, the biggest obstacle that most of us will meet on our journey is coming face-to-face with our own fears. We have so many fears drummed into us from the time that we are just small children – our fears of snakes, the dark, the unknown and the dentist are all very real when we are small (and for some of us, when we are large too!) – it's no wonder that so many people just won't do what needs to be done.

The two main fears that you will face on your wealth journey are the fear of failure and the fear of success.

The fear of failure can absolutely paralyse. Deal with it by understanding that there is only one kind of failure and that is the failure to participate. If you are out there doing what you need to do to get whatever it is that you want, it doesn't matter how many times you get a 'no' or a result that is not what you expected. Anthony Robbins says, 'There are no failures, only outcomes'. Look at this fear coldly and analytically. If you completely screw up and lose everything, will you go to gaol? Probably not. If you started from nothing, what have you really lost?

The fear of success can be even more devastating than the fear of failure. What if you are out there hunting down great deals, making money and living the life of your dreams? All of a sudden, you are not meeting the expectations of others and you are no longer 'normal' – if normal means arriving at retirement at age 65 broke and on a pension, then I choose not to be normal.

You cannot deal with any kind of fear by running from it, ignoring it or trying to rationalise it away. You must confront it head-on. Break down your fear piece-by-piece and deal with it one chunk at a time.

Apart from real estate, are there any other asset classes that you invest in?

In my early twenties all I ever thought about was property and I probably had about 95% of my net wealth stored there. I didn't know much about shares or business, so to me they were too risky.

After having learnt that property can go down as well as up, I learnt about the benefits of spreading my investments across different asset classes. I also learnt that while property is strong, it does have its weaknesses that shares can make up for. If you take a look at the BRW Rich List you'll find that there are many people who have made significant wealth through their own businesses or by acquiring a large amount of stock in other companies. I now invest about 50% of my total wealth in real estate, 30% in businesses (including what I do at Aspire International) and short term

> **The future belongs to those who see the possibilities before they become obvious.**

property investments through developing and refurbishing. The final 20% is held in cash, shares and options, which are fairly liquid and the options generate significant income each month. This spread is ideal for me at this time in my life. Yours will vary dramatically according to your individual risk profile, age and of course, what you like to put your money into.

Are there any significant quotes that you live your life by?

There are many, in fact I could probably fill a book with them. I spend a great deal of time soaking up all the wisdom I can from people like Jim Rohn and Anthony Robbins. I read extensively and often copy down sayings that catch my attention. Often I find that a saying might not mean much to me until I am ready and open to understanding the message within the words, so having them recorded means I can go back and review them when I am looking for inspiration.

One of the quotes I like is made up from other speakers, with a little of my own wisdom added in, 'Life is what you make it, never miss anything. It is in your dreams that your life begins'. This quote is all about being responsible for your life, learning from the past, living in the now and planning for the future.

What do you see as the major investment opportunities over the next ten to twenty years?

It's my opinion that we will see some dramatic changes in demographics in the coming years. Smaller household sizes will mean that people want fewer bedrooms and larger living areas. There will be high demand for well-located property (near lifestyle and entertainment facilities) on smaller, low-maintenance blocks. I've seen a continuing trend back to inner city living by people who are selling their homes in the suburbs and choosing to be where the action is, in a secure environment that they can lock up and leave when they go travelling.

On the flip side, there will be another shift from capital cities to coastal towns and centres. This move started 30 years ago on the Gold Coast in Queensland and continues today, particularly along the eastern seaboard of Australia. Prices in those areas will keep moving upward. And it's not just the retirees making the move; more than 80% of people moving to the coast are under the age of 50. These are people who are more mobile, willing to telecommute and many have been frozen out of the big city home ownership markets.

Security will be another big issue and I see the coming of planned estates that are walled with entry gates and 24-hour security. You'll need a pass to get in and out of these places and I guarantee that demand for these 'safe' suburbs will be high.

One of my favourite sayings is, 'The future belongs to those who see the possibilities before they become obvious'. I have just given you a look at future trends that will richly reward those who supply the market. What will you do with this information?

What are some of your plans or goals for the next five years?

From a business perspective, my company, Property Millionaire Pty Ltd, has successfully operated in a purely investment education environment – we have books, audio CDs and various home-study packs offering different levels of property investment learning. Our thousands of readers and graduates are now asking us to widen our services to provide more than just education. Some of these new services will include loan broking, mentoring groups, property search, property management, syndications and possibly even financial planning with a bias towards direct investing rather than just managed funds. For this we have adopted a new name, Aspire International, and a new business culture that incorporates all of the above and more.

On a personal level, I plan to release more books, do more speaking both nationally and internationally, become involved in more property developments and spend more time travelling the world with my partner.

FREE BONUS GIFT

Craig Turnbull has kindly offered a FREE BONUS GIFT valued at $35.00 to all readers of this book...

47 Tips and Tricks for Property Success – In this fun and extremely informative eBook, Craig Turnbull shares 47 tips and tricks compiled during his twenty-year property career. Jam-packed with useful ideas, this eBook will save you thousands of dollars and fast-track your path to financial freedom.

Simply visit the website below and follow the directions to download direct to your Notebook or PC.

www.SecretsExposed.com.au/property_millionaires

A SENSE OF URGENCY

Patrick Bright

PATRICK BRIGHT

> " I don't understand why people make property more complicated than it is; this formula could be taught to a twelve-year-old kid – so get moving! "

PATRICK BRIGHT

Patrick (Pat) Bright was born in the Sydney suburb of Normanhurst in 1974. Together with his sisters, he grew up under the guidance of firm but fair parents who expected their children to pitch in. Almost as soon as he was old enough to hold a hammer, he was put to work helping his builder father around the house and on building sites.

At the age of fifteen, Pat left school to become a carpenter – he had observed that wealthy people own real estate and figured that if he wanted to become wealthy, he should learn how to build houses. He soon realised that he didn't need to know how to build houses, just how to buy and sell them, so he became a real estate selling agent.

Life as a real estate sales agent left Pat feeling disenchanted with the industry and he decided to move on. While considering his next career move, he did a few favours by locating suitable properties for friends and ex-colleagues looking to buy. Before he knew it he was busy buying homes, investments and commercial properties. Although Pat didn't know it at the time, he was pioneering the relatively new field of real estate buyers' agents in Australia.

Since then Pat has personally negotiated to buy several hundred properties for both himself and his clients – everything from a $53,000 apartment to a $20 million residential subdivision. His real estate buyers' agency, EPS Property Search, is recognised as a leader in this fast-growing sector.

Pat is a best-selling author and has been featured in dozens of newspaper articles and radio programs. Today he lives in Sydney's Neutral Bay and when he isn't working, you'll find him on the golf course, raising money for charities or tearing around Eastern Creek Raceway in his Porsche.

Why did you decide to start investing in property?

I decided at a young age to become wealthy, so I studied the habits of rich people and what I found was that most wealthy people had either made or stored their wealth in property. The more I looked into it, the more I realised that property investment was the best and safest way to create and hold onto wealth.

My approach is 'safety and wealth through property investment', not high-risk 'get rich quick' schemes – I want to hang onto my shirt and be able to sleep at night. A few years ago I did a number of 'get rich quick' style courses and became so pumped up that I thought I was going to make loads of money fast. I later realised that it takes a little bit of careful planning and some time. Get rich a little slower and hang on to it, that's my recommendation.

What do you love about property?

Essentially, there are three main things you can choose to invest in: business, shares and property. Following are just a few points why I believe that property is the best and safest way to create long-term wealth:

- Property offers consistent capital growth. On average, over the last 100 years, Sydney real estate has grown by just over 10% per annum – with compound growth, a property doubles in value every 7.2 years.
- Unlike shares and businesses, property isn't subject to extreme price fluctuations.
- Property can be bought at a discount.
- It's easy to add value to your property investment. You can't do much to improve the value of your Woolworths shares apart from shop there, a lot.
- Property offers a variety of generous tax benefits.
- Property can be leveraged easier and more than other investments.
- It's easy and cheap to insure.

> **In the USA and Europe buyers' agents are just as common as selling agents.**

What is a buyers' agent and what exactly do they do?

A proper real estate buyers' agent is a licensed real estate professional who works exclusively for buyers, helping them to search for, negotiate and purchase suitable properties.

Really good buyers' agents have systems that enable them to canvas the whole marketplace and access all properties for sale, including the 'silent sales' (properties that are not publicly on the market). Through intensive comparative market analysis, we're able to determine a fair market price for a property, which enables us to identify good deals. We then show our buyers a selection of properties matched to their exact criteria, and when it's time to buy, we negotiate on our clients' behalf, getting them the best possible price and the most favourable terms and conditions. A real buyers' agent gives the buyer the upper hand by having an experienced real estate negotiator on their side – the bottom line is, by using a buyers' agent you save a whole lot of your own time, money and stress.

In the USA and other parts of the world buyers' agents are just as common as selling agents. In Australia, the industry is still in its infancy, but it is gaining exposure and growing through word-of-mouth. In today's demanding and time-poor society it makes sense to recruit a buyers' agent to take care of your property interests, just as you would hire an accountant to look after your finances and a lawyer to take care of your legal requirements.

Why should people consider using a buyers' agent?

I think the biggest reason is the savings. Typically, our clients save in excess of 5% on the fair market value of their property purchases – not to mention what often ends up being hundreds of hours in search time.

Some clients have never bought a property before, so they come to me because they find the property market daunting and don't want to make a costly mistake. What I do in these cases is educate them as I guide them through the entire buying process, from searching for a suitable property to signing the contract of sale, right up until I hand them the keys to their new property on settlement day. Many of my other clients are sophisticated investors or busy professionals who simply don't have enough time to search for property. Some are looking for renovation projects but don't have the time to search for themselves because they are busy with current renovations. Others come to me because they're thinking about retirement and want to start up an investment portfolio. For industrial and commercial clients, I have been able to locate suitable properties for their businesses with little interruption to their day-to-day operations.

Patrick with investor clients Sue and Simon.

> **I decided to buy the property knowing that I might end up with the business as well.**

What fees are involved and what do people get for their money?

There are a handful of buyers' agents out there, some charge a flat fee, some charge a percentage of the sale price. The fees usually depend on the client's particular needs and the level of service they require. The best thing to do is sit down with a good buyers agent and run through all the details of the type of property you require. Only then will they be able to give you a quote for their services. Personally, I am extremely confident of saving my clients at least my fee (and often far more than that) through negotiating the best possible price and terms on their behalf.

Though each company's services will differ, here's a brief summary of what our 'Search, Research and Negotiation Service' covers:

- An initial consultation to discuss and evaluate the client's specific requirements and 'wish list'.
- Intensive search and research to find suitable properties.
- Development of a shortlist of suitable properties and private inspections.
- A comprehensive comparative market analysis to determine the fair market value of the properties the client chooses from the shortlist.
- Negotiation on purchase price, terms and conditions.
- Co-ordination of building and pest inspections.
- Finding tenants through our property management department, if required.

What's one of the best deals you've ever done and why did it work so well?

I've been playing the property game for more than ten years now and I've done several deals that I would consider to be pretty outstanding. However, one of my better deals was buying a commercial carwash site. The landlord wanted to sell because he wasn't getting the rent on time. On top of that, the carwash business was struggling – the owner was tired of it and it looked like it would fail sooner rather than later. I decided to buy the property knowing that I might end up with the business as well. The landlord agreed to my offer because he was fed up with the tenant hassles and wanted to get out fast. I bought the site with a 34% rental yield. As I had assumed, the business failed and in conjunction with another guy, I took over the carwash business, fixed it up and resold it for a profit. While we were fixing up the business I renegotiated the lease with myself to get an even higher yield. A year after I bought it, I refinanced the site and pulled out a few hundred thousand dollars, which I used to buy another property without having to use any of my own money.

That was a dream deal. It took a bit of creative thinking and patience to line everything up, but it was well worth it.

When do you think is the best time for someone to start investing in property?

The best time to start investing in property is as soon as you can afford it. You've got to understand, the property market grows faster than you can save so you're not likely to ever catch it. Over the last 100, Sydney property has grown, on average, 10% every year. That means the size of the deposit necessary to buy a property grows by 10% each year as well – so your savings target keeps expanding by 10% of the current value of the property you're interested in each year, which is not something that many people can keep up with.

So where are you going to get that extra money from? If you're serious about buying an investment property you're probably already saving at your limit and you can't rely on wage increases to keep pace with the market. Between 1996 and 2003 house prices in Sydney rose by 100%, but average weekly earnings rose by only 3.6% per annum over that same period. The only way to keep up with the property market is to be *in* the property market.

What do you say to people who think it is too late for them to get into the market?

Get started right now. Take action! Do something! It's better to do something than to do nothing.

Take a moment to consider the consequences of doing nothing. As I mentioned earlier, Sydney property goes up in value roughly 10% every year. Due to the magic of compound interest, that means a property will double in value in 7.2 years. Take a $300,000 property for example:

Year	Property Value	Capital Growth
1	$300,000 × 10% = $330,000	$ 30,000
2	$330,000 × 10% = $363,000	$ 63,000
3	$363,000 × 10% = $399,000	$ 99,000
4	$399,000 × 10% = $439,000	$139,000
5	$439,000 × 10% = $483,000	$183,000
6	$483,000 × 10% = $531,000	$231,000
7	$531,000 × 10% = $584,000	$284,000
8	$584,000 × 10% = $643,000	$343,000

After seven years, a $300,000 property is worth $584,000, meaning the capital growth is $284,000. There are 364 weeks in seven years (7 × 52), so the value of the property is growing at a rate of $780 per week on average. If you invest in property in Sydney, that's what you can make every week just by sitting on your butt! That's what you're missing out on every week that you delay getting into the market. If you're looking at purchasing a property for $400,000, the weekly capital growth you're missing out on is around $1,100 and at $500,000, it's costing you $1,370 per week – that's more than the average Australian income, for doing nothing apart from signing your name to a piece of paper.

Now do you have a sense of urgency?

What do you think are the most common mistakes new investors make?

I think the most common mistake is not doing enough research. A recent *60 Minutes* report conservatively estimated that 250,000 Australians have been stung by property scams in the last ten years alone. These are mostly people from Sydney and Melbourne who've been flown up to the Gold Coast where they signed up for investment property deals that were just too good to be true. Many bought property, sight-unseen, from unethical financial planners or property marketing companies with nothing more than glossy brochures. Without a well researched point of reference all of the figures probably seemed very attractive, but the punters ended up paying well above fair market value – in some cases as much as 50% more than what the property was worth. At the end of the day, you just have to do your research.

Another common mistake is to let your emotions drive your financial decisions. While I was working as a selling agent I saw many buyers get overly emotional about a property and end up paying far too much for it. To stop myself from becoming over emotional as an investor I drew up a set of rules and decided what I would and would not accept when I was considering a deal. If a property failed to meet even one of my criteria I wouldn't buy it.

As a guide, how many properties should someone look at before purchasing one?

To get an accurate picture of fair market value, I recommend looking at roughly 100 properties that are comparable to the one you would like to buy. Why do I suggest 100 properties? Well, if you only see 50, you're probably not well enough informed. If you see 150, I don't think you would be that much better informed and

> ❝ A recent *60 Minutes* report conservatively estimated that 250,000 Australians have been stung... ❞

it's a lot of extra work. From my experience, 100 properties are enough for the average person to be on the ball about comparative prices in an area.

When I'm looking for a property for a client, I still do the legwork and inspect around 100 properties, especially if I haven't purchased in that area recently. I've bought properties all over Australia, in all different price ranges and I always stick to the 100 properties formula. In fact, you could drop me anywhere in the world, give me enough time to inspect 100 properties and I can assure you that I won't be paying retail when I buy.

Try it for yourself. Even if you're working full-time, make a decision to block out a few hours every Saturday and aim to see five or ten properties. If you're doing this with your partner or family, perhaps make a day of it and take a break for a picnic lunch in the park. If you're consistent, you will have seen 100 properties in approximately two or three months, making you an expert in that area and giving you an advantage over 98% of the competition. You will be able to identify real bargains instantly and come from a no-need position when negotiating, because you know another deal is just around the corner.

I don't understand why people make property more complicated than it is; this formula could be taught to a twelve-year-old year old kid – so get moving!

In which areas do you recommend people buy their investment properties?

This is where most people come across a roadblock. I believe that *where* you buy should always be determined by *why* you're buying. That's why your individual wealth creation strategy is key.

What is your personal wealth creation strategy and why do you take this approach?

Even though I do own rural and commercial property, right now I prefer to invest in high capital growth residential property. I'm always looking for an area that has potential for above-average growth in the future. While I am interested in what's been happening over the past five years, I'm even more interested in what's going to happen in the next ten. I look for areas that haven't done much for a while, that are primed for capital growth due to upcoming redevelopment or increases in demand arising from changing lifestyles and demographics.

I also invest in businesses. I like to buy, build and sell them. It's very challenging but I enjoy it and have taken the time to understand what makes a business successful. I like investing in businesses because I can have control over them and can add value to my investment. At this stage I choose not to invest in the share market because I have no control over what happens.

What are the most important lessons you've learnt about property investing?

The first thing is that you make your money when you buy. If you pay retail it really slows you down when you're trying to build your wealth or get into the next deal. If you buy a property and can't sell it the very next day for more than you paid for it, then I believe you've paid too much.

Another very important factor in becoming a successful property investor is doing your research. If you're going to 'work' as a property investor then you need to understand the industry. You need to educate yourself about the 'ins and outs' as well as the pros and cons of property investment. More specifically, when you're planning to buy a property you need to do a comprehensive comparative market analysis to make sure you're getting a good deal.

> **❝ I look for areas that haven't done much for a while, that are primed for capital growth due to upcoming redevelopment or increases in demand. ❞**

What advice would you give to someone who wants to get started in property investing?

My advice to people starting out is to treat property investment as a serious hobby or even like a real business. You've got to make a commitment to being a real investor, which means consistently devoting your time, energy and passion to it. You've got to know what you're doing and why. Do you do it because it interests you and you enjoy the thrill of the deal? Or is it because of the financial security it brings? Either way, you've got to know your 'why'.

What are some of the methods you use to leverage your time when looking for investment opportunities?

One of my techniques is what I call the 'Fast Track Super Search'. Basically, I create a contact database of all the selling agents in the area I'm interested in. I contact each office and each individual agent and qualify suitable properties over the phone so I don't waste time looking at unsuitable ones. This is also a great way to hear about silent or potential off-market purchases. It enables me to quickly sift through the whole marketplace so I don't miss any quality property.

How do you go about finding properties below market value?

There are two main factors that will enable you to buy property below market value, they are: extensive research and negotiation skills.

I canvas every single selling agent in the area I'm interested in buying in to make sure I've covered every property for sale and I do a thorough comparative market analysis to get an accurate picture of current market values. This research helps me to uncover undervalued properties, and then I use my negotiation skills to get the best possible deal. My negotiation skills come from a combination of real estate experience, intuition and knowledge of the tricks of the trade I have picked up over the years. I don't have a 'set-in-stone' negotiation procedure because each transaction and the parties involved are slightly different. Key to any negotiation is finding out how motivated the vendor is to sell – a vendor selling under pressure is usually more flexible on price and terms. More often than not I negotiate different terms and conditions to the original contract to move the focus of the negotiations away from the price. You have to learn how to tailor your negotiations to each individual purchase.

As a buyers' agent I believe I have certain advantages over the average purchaser. For example, because I'm not buying the property for myself, my emotions are completely removed from the negotiation, allowing me to be far more objective and relaxed. And as a bonus, selling agents know that I have a number of buyers at any one time, and they'll often let me know about properties they have just listed but not yet advertised to the general market. This gives me a foot in the door to quickly seize new opportunities.

I explain many other techniques for finding discounted properties in my book, *The Insider's Guide to Buying Real Estate*. Through experience, I know that if you are conscientious about your research and follow the system for buying property, you will never have to pay above market value. And, if you're a confident negotiator and take advantage of all the negotiation tactics I share in my book, you'll seriously save thousands.

Is it true that many of the best deals are purchased before they even go on the public market?

Yes, in fact 38% of the properties my buyer's agency purchased for our clients in 2002/2003 never hit the public market. You might think that the vendor gets top dollar if their home doesn't go on the open market, and sometimes that's true, but often it's the case that the vendor has said to the agent, 'If you can get me X dollars for my home then I will sell, otherwise I am not interested in selling'. There are many other reasons why the vendor might be willing to give you a good deal for a quick sale. First up, the vendor saves a big chunk of cash on advertising that may or may not work. And, if they have to sell in a hurry, as the majority of vendors do because of death, divorce, another purchase, relocation, bridging finance or because the bank said, 'Sell it or we will do it for you', the quick turnaround is a

> **Novice negotiators often don't realise that the terms and conditions of the contract of sale are just as important (and sometimes even more important) as the price.**

big plus – just one of these factors can literally save you tens of thousands of dollars. And believe it or not, some people just don't want the hassle of two-to-three months of cleaning up daily for private inspections and open houses. They just want the whole process to be quick, quiet and hassle-free.

What are some of your favourite negotiation techniques when buying property?

Novice negotiators often don't realise that the terms and conditions of the contract of sale are just as important (and sometimes even more important) than the price. The key to successful negotiation is in finding out what the other party wants and giving it to them – as long as you also get what you want, of course. By negotiating terms and conditions that are favourable to the vendor you can add value to the deal without actually paying any more cash. In fact, when I offer certain terms, I usually get further discounts on the purchase price.

One of the best areas to negotiate is the settlement period. To make this work, you'll need to find out when the vendor wants to move. Do they want to move in six, eight or ten weeks? What timeframe will suit them best? If they've bought somewhere else and are keen to move on, offer them a four-week settlement or if they want time to find another home, offer them ten weeks, provided they'll knock a few thousand dollars off the price.

Do you prefer to buy at auctions?

The auction selling strategy is promoted by selling agents as the best way to get the highest possible price. From my experience this is not necessarily the case. On many occasions I have purchases property at auctions well below what I was prepared to pay, and well below its market value. On the other hand, the high-pressure atmosphere can stimulate other bidders desire to own the property. Heightened emotions create competition, and competition fuels most people's desire to win. As a result, people often end up paying more than they planned and certainly more than the property is really worth.

I'm not anti-auction, in fact I enjoy the thrill of the bidding process, but I'd prefer to negotiate a price before auction. That way I can negotiate the terms and conditions I want, at the price I want. Plus, at the end of the day, if I really want the property, buying it prior reduces the risk of being out bid at the auction.

Having bought hundreds of properties at auctions and being a trained auctioneer yourself, what are some of the tricks you use to outsmart the competition?

There are several bidding strategies that I use depending on the circumstances. I've named one the 'Knock-out Bid' and this is great for taking the momentum out of an auction. For example, say I've done my research and I know the property is worth at least $500,000 and could end up going for more. And let's say the bidding starts at $300,000 and is going up first in $20,000 bids and then $10,000 bids. At the $400,000 mark I will call out $450,000, and in many cases it will stop the auction dead. More often than not, it will then take the auctioneer some work to get the bidding going again. If there are inexperienced bidders at the auction it can blow them away. They get all nervous because they think you're a professional and you know what you're doing, which is exactly what I want. I have done this many times and sometimes no further bids are made and the property is passed in or knocked down (sold) to me at that point.

As a professional exclusive buyers' agent, my confidence and experience can intimidate other buyers as well as the auctioneer. I keep the auctioneer honest because he or she knows that I'm not afraid to hold them accountable for any bids they take. I want them thinking about me and what I might do next and not about the other bidders.

There are loads of companies out there that claim to find 'hot deals' for investors. How do you know which ones are offering real value and which are taking you for a ride?

It's often very hard to pick them, because they have become very good at disguising themselves. In short I don't recommend buying from 'spruikers' at property seminars, financial planners, over the internet or in another country without throughly checking out the property deals yourself. It's just laziness on your part and if you're lazy, you'll very likely get burnt. Also, never buy property through anyone that you're not paying to act in your best interests. If they're not a licensed exclusive real estate buyers' agent with the Department of Fair Trading (or your states equivalent government body) you're still quite exposed to being taken for a ride. Remember, if *you're* not paying them they're being paid by someone else, so they're acting in the vendor's interests and not yours.

Who are the mentors that have inspired you, and what important lessons have you learnt from them?

Dolf de Roos was one of my early influences; he was the first person to explain property investment to me in a practical, no-nonsense way. He taught me not to be afraid of debt. Essentially what he said was, 'all you're doing is signing your name on a piece of paper to control an asset that will grow and repay you many times over' – now that isn't so scary, is it?

Gordon Green was another of my early mentors. I had heard about him and was fortunate enough to hear him speak at a seminar. Like me, he had a building industry background. What I liked about him was that even though he had more than 30 years' experience in the game, he didn't feel the need to talk himself up or act like a high-flyer. I was really impressed by his wisdom and practical, no-nonsense, down-to-earth approach. One of Gordon's favourite sayings was, 'Borrow as much as you can, from whomever you can, whenever you can, for as long as you can, provided you can sleep at night'. He also advised that you should never gear your portfolio over 80%, in fact it is best to keep it closer to 60%, I think this is sensible advice because then you've always got some cash in reserve to do other deals, and if interest rates move up on you unexpectedly there's room to refinance if you need to.

Are there any significant quotes that you live your life by?

'The deal of the decade comes around once a week'. If you keep your eye out and do your research you'll find plenty of good deals. If a deal doesn't meet my numbers and my rules I don't get upset about it because I know there'll be another one next week.

I'm also guided by the law of karma, 'What I put out comes back – often ten fold'. It's my frim belief that if I'm good to people then people and life will be good to me. That's why it's extremely important for you to aim for the highest standards of honesty and integrity in both your professional and private life at all times.

If anyone can succeed in property no matter what their current financial circumstances are, what do you think holds people back from becoming property millionaires?

To be a successful investor you have to be able to withstand short-term pain to achieve long-term gain. A lot of people don't have the discipline to deny themselves in the short term, so they find it difficult to get into a consistent savings habit. I find the challenge for most people is that they would rather *look* rich than *be* rich. They would rather travel, drive flash cars, eat at fancy restaurants, wear designer clothes, shout their mates rounds of $15 cocktails and then complain about how hard it is to save and get into the property market.

Life is full of choices. Personally, I believe it's far better to become wealthy first, then drive the fancy cars and take the overseas holidays. Earlier in my life I had very bad spending habits, but I learnt that you need to make some sacrifices in order to become financially independent. I owned five properties before I purchased a car worth more than $12,500, and I always pay cash for my cars. I'll always remember my father's advice, 'Son, never finance a depreciating asset unless someone else is paying for it'.

What do you see as the major investment opportunities over the next ten to twenty years?

You will always do well with residential property because people will always need a place to live. One of the biggest impacts on the property market over the next fifteen years will be the baby boomers retiring on mass. Retiring baby boomers will want to remain reasonably active and they don't want to spend their weekends doing lawns and gardens. They don't need a four-bedroom home because there's only the two of them now the kids have moved out. They want low-maintenance, high-convenience property, close to the beach, the city, cafés, restaurants, theatres and cinemas. As the baby boomer consumer machine turns its attention to coastal and inner-city café-lifestyle properties, the demand for apartments and townhouses will skyrocket. That's why I believe that for residential property investment, the growth areas of the future will be in quality well positioned townhouses and boutique apartments.

FREE BONUS GIFT

Patrick Bright has kindly offered a FREE BONUS GIFT valued at $22.95 to all readers of this book…

11 Power-Packed Strategies For Negotiating – Over the last few years, leading buyers' agent Patrick Bright has purchased over $300 million worth of real estate for his many clients. In this special report you'll learn eleven tried and tested strategies for negotiating the best deal every time. Apply just one of these strategies successfully and you can save tens of thousands of dollars on your next property purchase.

Simply visit the website below and follow the directions to download direct to your Notebook or PC.

www.SecretsExposed.com.au/property_millionaires

CREATING THE CASH COW

Dymphna Boholt.

DYMPHNA BOHOLT

> ❝ It is a whole lot easier to be a successful property investor than to be a successful mum. But being a mum is a whole lot more rewarding. ❞

PROFILE

DYMPHNA BOHOLT

Dymphna Boholt was born in a small central Queensland town in 1963. She has a natural entrepreneurial spirit – her first investment, at the age of four, was a cow which she bred with others to create her first asset portfolio, a herd.

Dymphna graduated from the Australian National University in Canberra with a degree in economics and accounting and then moved to Sydney to take up a position with Coopers & Lybrand (one of the 'big eight' accountancy firms in the world at that time). In 1994 she moved to the Sunshine Coast where she found herself starting over after a divorce had left her with very little and two toddlers to support. She began her own accountancy practice, Active Financial Answers, which today is a thriving business based in Maroochydore with offices in Melbourne and Sydney.

In 2000 Dymphna met US property guru and real estate adviser to Robert Kiyosaki, Dolf de Roos. She was so inspired by his teachings that she began to learn how to invest in real estate as a way of generating cash flow and creating long-term wealth. Within just three years she had accumulated a $3.5 million property portfolio, with $1.55 million in equity.

Dymphna is dedicated to showing others how to achieve financial freedom through education and planning and is in great demand both nationally and internationally as a speaker on how to grow wealth through property investment. She is the co-founder of WildlyWealthyWomen.com and the Millionaire Mentoring Program, and is regarded as one of Australia's leading asset protection and taxation specialists.

She is happily married and has three children.

Why did you decide to start investing in property?

Like many people, I'd always been very busy coping with the challenges and stress of day-to-day life without giving too much thought to the future. It took a major event to make me take a step back and really look at where my life was going. For me, this was the trauma of going through an emotional divorce. I found myself alone for the first time in more than ten years with a baby to care for and another on the way. Reality had struck!

Even though I had been successful in the past, having children to support is a whole new reality. My first thoughts were of survival and my security blanket was what I knew best: business, economics and accounting. I needed the flexibility of being able to work around raising my children so I chose to set up my own accountancy practice rather than take on a J.O.B. (Just Over Broke).

I moved to the beautiful Sunshine Coast and walked the streets introducing myself to local business owners in the hope of securing clients for my new practice, Active Financial Answers. This approach was completely unheard of in the very conservative world of financial professionals, even more so considering that I was heavily pregnant at the time. But whether out of sympathy or admiration for my 'guts' to get out there, clients joined my practice and over the next few years it grew to a level where I was earning a reasonable income. Even so, I was still only trading my time for money.

I realised that I had a choice to make: I could continue on this path, work hard and end up with a successful practice and a moderate amount of money saved for my retirement, or I could step outside my comfort zone and take a chance on having some of that retirement lifestyle a whole lot sooner.

I knew that I would need an income that came in regardless of whether I worked or didn't; I needed a passive income – the ability to literally earn money while I slept. Property investment provided the ideal solution. But

> **I needed a passive income – the ability to literally earn money while I slept.**

not just any property – it had to be the right type of property, what I call a 'Cash Cow Property'. That is, a property that produces more income through rent than it requires in outgoing costs. Good examples of cash cow properties include dual occupancies, dual use properties, blocks of units, regional properties, small shopping centres and warehouse complexes.

This is where the big adventure really began.

How do you recommend that people effectively balance long-term wealth creation with the need for immediate cash flow?

It's all about balance. Too many investors think that there is only one way to make money in the property market: growth – you buy a property, it goes up in value and you make money, right? Well that's one way, but it is certainly not the only way. In fact, it only works well in a rising market and as we all know, rising markets come and go in cycles.

What an astute investor should do is spend time analysing their current financial circumstances and determining the financial position they want to be in. Believe it or not, this is actually the most difficult thing to do. Most people never write down, or even really know what their specific goals are. If you don't know what results you want from your investment portfolio, or indeed from your life, how on earth can you possibly expect to achieve them?

Let me explain. If you're happy earning income in the way that you currently do, and simply require a build-up of wealth to fall back on when you stop earning income, then certain types of property investments will be better suited to you – such as those that produce capital growth and are in high or increasing demand areas, or those through which growth can be manufactured, such as small construction projects, subdivisions, strata titling, larger developments or renovations. The closer you can get to these types of investments being cash flow neutral, the better. What do I mean by 'cash flow neutral'? That's where the property produces a sufficient rental income to cover all of its expenses (including interest on borrowings, rates, insurances, maintenance and so on) after taking into account any tax concessions you may be entitled to for depreciation and other property-related deductions.

On the other hand, you may hate your current line of work or at least not want to continue with it for the long term. In this case you need to look for alternative sources of income. The types of properties that you would build into your portfolio include those that provide strong cash flow rather than growth. However, it is still important to focus some attention on growth, or more particularly, manufactured growth; this will provide the equity that gives you the ability to buy additional cash cow properties.

This may all sound very confusing, but it's not. You simply need to determine what type of property will suit your portfolio and provide you with your desired outcome – income, growth or a combination of the two.

When you started out, was your goal for income or growth?

It was a mixture. To start with I needed cash flow to replace the income I had been earning through my accountancy practice. Cash cow properties would fulfil my goal of having time to do all the things a young family requires, such as being able to take time out for sports days and family fun. So I concentrated on properties that had long term, sustainable yields. These mostly came in the form of whole blocks of units in quite remote areas where the demand for rental accommodation is high. One of these is a block of five units in Weipa, far north Queensland. It's not very pretty, but it's a real little gem! This property cost $250,000 and earns me over $28,000 every year. That's passive income! Just think about it, what would an extra $28,000 per year mean to you if you didn't have to work for it? And all it took was one property purchase.

I also had to do some manufactured growth deals, such as renovations, in order to generate enough equity to buy the next cash cow in the portfolio. This is why balance is so important. Without both income for serviceability and equity for security, your ability to borrow will be severely inhibited.

One manufactured growth deal was a major renovation which in hindsight took far too long to complete. We tried to do too much ourselves in an effort to save money and should have used more contract labour than we did. In the end it took longer and cost more than it should have and it delayed further cash cow purchases. But, we did make a profit of over $75,000 and transformed something completely uninhabitable (including the twelve-foot carpet snake and colony of rats living in the kitchen) into a neat little three-bedroom house. The equity created through this property enabled us to buy the next cash cow.

BEFORE

AFTER

Do you need to have significant savings behind you before you get into the market?

No, but if you don't, you might just have to work harder. You might need to be a little more creative in the way you buy property and with the types of properties you buy. You might even need to share a few deals along the way with others who will also benefit but may be financially stronger applicants for a loan. Remember, half of a good deal is better than no deal at all.

One of the girls in my Wildly Wealthy Women mentoring program is a single mum in a remote country area who started out with very little. She was able to purchase three properties in her area within the first four months of the program. One was a block of eight units with a positive passive income of over $36,000 per year. She bought this property in a joint venture with another lady who was also on her own but already had significant equity in her home. Together, they are strata titling and renovating the block. When it is complete, each will own four units and have a passive income of between $15,000 and $20,000 per year – and, they will have had a lot of fun along the way! The equity created out of this manufactured growth deal is expected to be around $150,000 to $200,000 each. Her other two properties are both renovation jobs and yes, that means some hard work. However, the results have certainly convinced her that it's worth it. In a very short period of time, these two properties have generated an additional $90,000 in created growth, and passive income of around $4,000 per year. If she wants to take it further, the next step with both of these properties would be to build or move additional dwellings onto the block.

These types of results can turn lives around quickly, but more than anything, it's people's attitudes and expectations that change. The knowledge that this woman has gained will stay with her forever. No divorce can ever take that away from her and hopefully she will not only continue to apply that knowledge for herself but go on to help others in her community and circle of friends to improve their lives as well. That's why I do the mentoring programs and seminars, in the hope that I am not just educating one group of people, but that through them I am educating their entire circle of family and friends.

Having grown up in the country yourself, do you believe that there are still opportunities for people living in rural areas to make money in property?

Absolutely. It reminds me of the book, *Acres of Diamonds,* by Russell H Conwell, what most country people don't realise is that they are surrounded by little gems, particularly if it is high-income yields that you're after. Quite often, regional councils are much easier to deal with and are more amenable to having money spent in their area for the betterment of the community. And there are often more opportunities in regional communities to acquire properties with multiple streams of income.

Do you believe that people should stay on the sidelines when the property market is in a slump?

Absolutely not. Money can be made in the property market regardless of whether or not it is rising. When the market is not rising, it's the educated investor who is still making money and quite often, this is the time when the most money is made.

If your only strategy is targeting a 10% growth yield (as is the case with many investors and educators), then you are going to be restricted when the market is not rising. You can no longer just turn up in the market and buy something, anything, and still make money – you need to be smarter than that. You need to understand your goals, your portfolio and your strategy. You need to balance income and growth purchases, and you need to create your own growth through manufactured means.

Any downturn in an economy is simply a shift in wealth; think about it. In a depression, do we really have any less money in the world? I could go into a long explanation of supply and demand, global economics and fractional banking systems, but I won't (phew, you say!), just understand that money simply changes hands from one group to another – from uneducated hands to educated hands. When I was in my late teens, a wealthy farmer told me that he made most of his money and purchased most of his land holdings when times were tough. At the time the impact of this statement didn't sink in, but it does now.

What do you love about property?

I believe that property is the safest, most tax efficient and flexible investment available:

- You can improve its value through either your own or others' physical efforts or knowledge.
- No other investment is going to give you a tax deduction for not spending any money – this might seem strange, but it's called depreciation.
- Property is the most forgiving investment. Even if you do make a very ordinary property purchase, in time it will go up in value.
- Property is the only investment you can leverage at 80% or higher. (Leverage can be an investor's greatest ally or their worst enemy if they

don't know how to use it and don't incorporate a risk management strategy into their investment portfolio.)
- You have total control over your investment and can be as creative and involved as you desire.
- Anyone of legal age can invest in property.

What do you think are the essential qualities of a successful property investor?

There's only one – determination. Everything else can be learnt.

How helpful has your accounting background been in analysing investment opportunities?

It has been useful at a very basic level. By that I mean in helping me to know whether a particular property investment is going to make a profit before and after tax or not. However, this is something that can be learnt easily and becomes second nature to anyone investing on a continual basis. There are also lots of tools and computer programs that can help people with this type of analysis. At the end of the day, I believe common sense is far more important than any degree or piece of paper. Continuous education in your chosen field of interest is what gets results.

We know that you are very big on asset protection, why do you believe it is such an important part of any investment plan?

I am risk-adverse and one of the risks associated with property ownership is the risk of being sued. Property-related lawsuits can come completely 'out of the blue' and can have a devastating effect on an individual's net wealth if all of their assets are exposed.

There have been many cases where individuals are sued as a result of what might seem to be a low-risk activity. For example, think about what could happen if you forgot to pay the registration or insurance on your car for a week – it's easy to imagine that happening, you simply overlook it and plan to pay it next week, along with all the other bills. But what if you had an accident that was your fault and someone was injured? That person would be within their rights to seek compensation, but if your car was unregistered or uninsured do you think your insurance company would foot the bill? Fat chance. And what if the compensation ran into the millions? Could your portfolio withstand it?

How do you hold your assets? Do you own them in your own name? Do you own them as joint tenants with your spouse, or as tenants in common with your spouse? Are your assets held in trust for the benefit of future generations? Do you know whether your insurance covers you for damages incurred by trespassers or other uninvited guests on your property? Are you aware of whether your property is insured for the correct value? I have seen some very nice people lose assets unnecessarily because their affairs were not structured correctly for asset protection.

What are some of the ways in which investors can protect their assets?

Anyone in business or with investments (particularly property) needs specialist advice on asset protection. This is not something that property investors should take lightly.

Structuring for asset protection is about separating your assets and liabilities so that at any one time only one asset is exposed to potential risk. Your structure should be flexible enough to be able to grow with you as your needs and portfolio grow. Your adviser should not only ask you what your current objectives and requirements are, but also about your future goals and plans.

> ❝ Continuous education in your chosen field of interest is what gets results. ❞

Each person's circumstances are different and what is right for one person can be completely wrong for another. I am currently writing a book on structuring for asset protection and have put together an audio and workbook series on this topic. Specialists in asset protection, such as my Active Financial Answers practice, can advise people in this area.

How do you know if you are really getting the right advice from your accountant or financial planner?

The most important thing is to recognise that *you* are the one that needs to make decisions for your own future and take total responsibility for your life.

Whether you're asking a lawyer about the legal aspects of a deal, an accountant about taxation and GST issues or a finance broker about your borrowing capacity, make sure they're all up to date with your goals and objectives. And, make sure they're keen property investors themselves who have their finger on the pulse of the market.

When it comes to your financial planner, ask their opinion on the opportunity cost of making a particular property investment, and what other opportunities are out there. If you're game, you might even want to ask them when they plan on retiring – if the answer is more than ten years, you might wish to find another adviser!

Once you have information from your advisers, sit back and analyse the facts. Recognise who has a vested interest in providing you with certain information, and then make up your own mind. You are the only one who is solely focused on your situation, your portfolio and your strategy 100% of the time.

If you had to start again with nothing, what would you do?

If I was starting with absolutely nothing the first thing I would do is to look for a deal that I could either joint venture or have vendor financed, where I could apply my knowledge and do the work to turn a project into a manufactured growth deal. When I found the deal, I'd do the numbers and present the project to either the vendor or a joint venture partner. They'd see a great return – one that they probably wouldn't have been able to get without my knowledge and physical effort. Some such opportunities might include properties that could be strata-titled, subdivided or have a minor development approval granted to create a dual occupancy. I would show the vendor how, instead of selling the property short and giving the next buyer most of the profit, they could work with me, I would do all of the work and split the additional profit with them.

Let me give you a hypothetical example. Let's say 'Mum and Dad' are selling their large block in a good location because they find it requires too much up-keep now that the kids have left home. After speaking with them, you find out that they really don't want to leave the area where all of their friends are, but in fact what they really want is a smaller house which requires less maintenance. As an astute property investor, I might go away and put together a business plan that would show them how they could have their smaller house on the same block, along with five others that would put money into their pockets. Clearly, what I would be doing is creating a win-win situation for both parties.

Alternatively, 'Mum and Dad' might want to sell and move to another area, and I could help them get a whole lot more for their property than it is currently worth. I would do my research on the area and find out how much development-approved blocks were going for and whether a development and building approval could be granted on this particular block. If it could, I would put the deal to the vendors saying something along these lines: 'You're selling your property for (let's say) $400,000, but if I were able to work with you and gain a development

> ❝ You are the only one who is solely focused on your situation, your portfolio and your strategy 100% of the time. ❞

> **I encourage my Wildly Wealthy Women to form their own support groups.**

approval for six to eight townhouses on your block, your property would be worth $600,000. I have the time, the knowledge and the expertise to make this happen, so why not give it a go? Let's delay the sale of your property for six months and if I succeed, we split the additional $200,000 that I have manufactured for you 50/50. If I don't succeed, you still have your property and if you still want to sell, you can – nothing ventured, nothing gained'.

Now to me that's fair. Both parties achieve more by working together.

Another way might be to find a vendor finance deal where you can purchase the property with very little and use your physical efforts to renovate and manufacture growth. You'll then be in a position to either refinance the property through the regular channels or sell it and pick up on the growth that you have created. This equity or cash could then be used to buy the next property, which might even be another similar deal. In fact, you could make a deal with a full-time vendor financier to do 50/50 splits on all their property renovations, thus putting money in their pockets as well as your own. Nothing ventured, nothing gained.

Making money in the real estate market is not about ripping people off. It's about problem solving and creating as many win-win situations as you can. Anyone who is selling a property has a problem – they have a property that they no longer need or want. Getting to the real reason why a property is being sold can often mean that you not only create a great deal for yourself, but that you can solve the vendor's problems at the same time. You never know when someone will say 'yes'. As a seasoned property investor, I would certainly consider all such deals.

How important has it been for you to have a supportive spouse with regard to your investing?

I am grateful every day for the support and encouragement that I receive from my husband, Brian, he truly is my 'Number One Fan'. But support and encouragement don't only come from a spouse – they can come in many forms. I encourage my Wildly Wealthy Women to form their own support groups. They get together to share knowledge and support each other's goals on a regular basis. Communicating with other like-minded individuals with similar goals and aspirations is important, particularly for women. It is this camaraderie and spirit of 'help your mate' that to some degree has been eroded in our modern society. I hope that we can rekindle this sentiment by encouraging one another so that people don't have to feel alone in their endeavours.

What are some of the ways that you teach your children to understand the world of money?

Every parent has a responsibility to teach their children as best they can, and financial common sense is one of the important teachings we should pass on. My kids use a manual financial management system to earn their pocket money. They learn the value of things and what it takes to save up for something they really want. They know the pain of just how many times they have to wash the dishes or clean the car to repay a loan (plus interest, of course) for something that they absolutely had to have but didn't have enough money to buy. And they see how, when they buy income-producing assets, more money comes in than goes out each week.

My two eldest children are now aged nine and ten and are just starting to search the internet for properties that produce a passive income. They email questions to real estate agents to confirm details and when they know all the specifics, they present the deal. If my husband and I, or other investor friends, buy the property they make a $1,000 referral fee. Obviously, not all of that money can be spent; a part of it must be saved for investment purposes.

They understand the wisdom behind renovating a property so that it can be rented for more money or sold at a profit. They understand what a profit is, how tax is payable on profits and why taxes needs to be paid to support the building of roads, hospitals, schools and the like.

I remember once, when my eldest was in second grade, I went to the school for a parent-teacher interview and was challenged by the teacher, 'Do you monitor or know what sort of material your son is reading?' You can imagine what was running through my mind! With great trepidation I replied, 'No, not really, why?' 'Well,' the teacher explained, 'for the last three weeks for 'read aloud' your son has insisted on reading excerpts from *The Instant Millionaire* to the Grade Two class – and I really don't think that's appropriate reading material for grade twos'. I can assure you this came as a great relief!

Reading, the desire for knowledge and the process of seeking knowledge are very valuable skills to teach your children. I have told many audiences and friends that I believe it is a whole lot easier to be a successful property investor than to be a successful mum. But being a mum is a whole lot more rewarding.

What words of wisdom do you have for budding property investors?

Know what you want. Learn as much as you can. Apply what you learn. Stay focused and determined. Know that you will achieve what you want, and just do it.

MILLIONAIRE IN A YEAR

JOHN FITZGERALD

> " We grossed over $150 million in land sales from that one parcel of land. Sweet deal – it's amazing what being bold and knocking on doors can do! "

PROFILE

JOHN FITZGERALD

One of five children, John Fitzgerald was born in Melbourne in 1963. When he was just eight years old, John lost his father in a fatal car accident. By his own account, he was a below-average student and as soon as he finished his secondary education, with $200 in his pocket, he hitchhiked to Queensland to begin his real estate career.

At seventeen, John was one of the youngest ever licensed agents, by eighteen he had syndicated over $5 million in developments, at nineteen he launched a national property magazine, *Property Weekly Update,* and he began JLF Corporation at the age of twenty. Since then, he has bought, sold and developed more than 5,000 properties and amassed an extensive property portfolio. Today, JLF Corporation consists of 22 companies with an annual turnover of $100 million.

John is the chairman and founding benefactor of the Toogoolawa Children's Home Ltd, which has fostered more than 100 children categorised as 'youth at risk' or wards of the state. In 1998 Toogoolawa established its first school for non-mainstream students with learning difficulties. John has been featured on the ABC's *Australian Story* for his work with Toogoolawa.

In 2000 he was awarded the Australian Sports Medal for his achievements in the sport of polo. He is also a keen hiker and twice a year runs outdoor education classes for youth at risk.

John has written two books, *We Can be Heroes* and the best-selling *Seven Steps to Wealth* and is a highly sought-after public speaker.

He lives with his wife and two children on Queensland's Gold Coast, where his office 'Custodian House' is also situated on a ten-acre riverfront campus.

Why did you decide to start investing in property?

First, the 'heart' answer. I started working in real estate as a salesman when I was just seventeen years old. I'd hitchhiked up to the Gold Coast in the midst of a property boom, and I knew immediately that I wanted to be a part of it. Being among real estate agents, property managers and developers, I realised that the people who really got ahead financially were the ones who threw themselves into property for the long term. I knew I had to be a player in the game and not just an observer or a middleman.

Second, the 'head' answer. Property stacks up phenomenally well compared with other asset classes. In terms of performance, even allowing for the ups and downs that we all hear about, the underlying trend shows steady growth – and the demand for residential property has to continue as the population grows. Then there's the leverage; with property you can usually borrow up to 90% of the value, which means that you can build wealth more or less from scratch.

In my late teens I'd set myself a goal of becoming a millionaire by the age of 25, and property looked like the best way to go about it!

What is your personal property investment strategy and why do you take this approach?

I have two modes of investment. One is a 'passive' structure, which we use in our Custodian Wealth Builders program. It's relatively low maintenance, essentially relying on basic homework, cash flow management, capital growth and duplication to bring in steady returns over time. I call it 'get rich slow'! In a nutshell, you buy affordable residential properties with high land value (meaning houses, not units) that have real growth potential and are in reliable rent locations. You use your equity growth to obtain further finance and gradually build up a portfolio of properties.

> **Sometimes you can't wait around – do your homework and then take the leap!**

Meanwhile, you offset your costs through rental income and the tax deductions associated with negative gearing and the depreciation of newer buildings. It's very nearly that simple. If *all* you did was acquire and rent out six medium-priced houses over the next ten to fifteen years (assuming 8% growth), you'd end up with net assets of somewhere over $2 million and a positive income of approximately $40,000 per annum.

My other mode is 'accelerated' wealth building, where I'm more active in making opportunities, contacts and deals. This is where vendor terms, subdivisions, re-zonings and developments come in. I once bought a block of land for $1.25 million, I put down a $10,000 deposit and borrowed 100% from the bank on settlement. I then improved the property's value and sold it six months later at a profit of approximately $2.8 million – hence the name 'accelerated' wealth building.

What's one of the best deals you've ever done and why did it work so well?

I still get a kick out of my first major subdivision. I was 22 years old and desperately in need of capital to fulfil my splendid plan of becoming a millionaire within the next three years. I went to Sydney and put the door-knocking skills I'd developed as a Gold Coast real estate agent to good use, asking people to loan me $3 million, unsecured. Finally, a development company stopped laughing long enough to ask me what I would do with the money. I told them that I'd buy land, up-zone it and on-sell it. They asked me for a proposal.

I scouted around and found a large subdivision being sold by a mortgagee in possession, with approval for 700 lots. I contacted the mortgagee and expressed an interest 'on behalf of a large buyer from Sydney' (well, it was *potentially* true). They agreed to sell on a twelve-month contract for $2.25 million. I took this to the developer and said, 'We can buy this for $2.25 million with a $250,000 deposit, and a twelve-month settlement period. During that time, I'll re-zone the property to increase the yield from 700 to 1,200 lots, then we can on-sell it for $5.5-6 million'. I agreed to pay them 20% interest on their outlay, plus 50% of the profits – the other half was mine. The deal was done and I've never looked back.

It turned out that the developer and I became long term business partners and developed those 1,200 lots ourselves. We grossed over $150 million in land sales from that one parcel of land. Sweet deal – it's amazing what being bold and knocking on doors can do!

When do you think is the best time for someone to start investing in property?

I suppose there is a technical answer to this question to do with counter-cyclical buying, which is about picking up prime opportunities at the low point of a property market downturn so that you reap the rewards on the upswing, but ask a hundred punters and you'll get a hundred different views on where we are at in the cycle and what to do about it. The fact is that it is *always* possible to find real opportunities for capital growth, if you know what to look for.

The best time to start investing in property is *right now*. Too many people put it off, waiting for the ideal conditions or more certainty. I sometimes tell the story of the impala, an amazing animal I saw once when I was in Africa. An impala can jump up to twelve feet high, but in a zoo environment it can be kept behind a fence that's no more than four feet high. Why? Because an impala won't jump over anything if it can't see where its feet are going to land. Sometimes people are like impalas in that they require too much certainty before they take the leap. Remember, Colonel Sanders got going at the age of 65. Sometimes you can't wait around – do your homework and then take the leap!

What criteria do you use to select investment properties for sustained capital growth?

In my passive wealth building structure, I use pretty rigorous criteria, not only for sustained capital growth but also for 'rentability' to support my cash flow. First and foremost, I look for at least 40% land content, which means a house or a duplex. I look for affordable properties because they are less sensitive to market fluctuations and show reliable demand. I also look for (or develop) new buildings because of the potential for depreciation on houses built after 1985; this really makes a big difference to cash flow. In terms of location, I look for:

- Growth trends in population and employment.
- Proximity to a CBD and infrastructure (transport, shops, jobs, schools, recreation and so on).
- A secure, family-oriented area where at least 70% of households are owner-occupied, with an average of three or more people per household.
- A high, established capital benchmark which reflects the potential value of property in the area
- Room for growth. The median house price must be affordable in relation to average income in the area so that owners (and banks) can support higher borrowing levels when growth does occur.

In my accelerated wealth building, I'm more focused on spotting the potential in an asset that is currently under-valued or under-utilised. I can then add value and bring the property up to its highest potential rental or resale value.

Cash flow is important to your investment strategy, how do you ensure a steady flow of rental income?

The simplest answer is to select a good property manager, communicate with him or her regularly and encourage them to communicate regularly with you!

I use property managers who are focused full-time on rental properties. Selling can be more profitable than running a rental roll, so often you'll find agents who only manage properties part-time. You want a person who puts *all* their time and energy into rentals, not selling.

I also check that the property manager is experienced in administering a significant rental roll, has a low rental vacancy rate and a good computer system for tracking things such as overdue rents, property inspections and tenant credit checks.

I have a policy of charging slightly under market rates of rent. Prospective tenants will often go for a discounted rate and even appreciate it. In return, I find I get a degree of loyalty and co-operation from tenants. At the end of the day, $10 per week off your bottom line income is a small price to pay for a comparatively hassle-free tenancy, particularly when you are the landlord of four or five properties.

I must add, despite the horror stories and urban myths, I haven't had that many bad experiences with tenants. I take basic precautions such as getting prospective tenants properly checked out, keeping an eye on overdue rents, maintaining inspections and taking out landlord protection insurance, it's worth it!

In your books, you talk about bank valuations, lending criteria and cross-collateralisation policies. What do you look for in a lender?

If you're buying one investment property it may not matter too much, but if you are looking to build a property portfolio, you need a lender that will work with you. From the outset I establish that I intend to use the increased equity in a property to build an investment portfolio, most of

> " At the end of the day, $10 per week off your bottom line income is a small price to pay for a comparatively hassle-free tenancy... "

the important questions and decisions flow from there. I have three criteria when choosing a lender:

1. To start with, I'm looking for a lender that will offer me a 90% loan value ratio (LVR) on an investment property. This means that once my asset grows in value by say 10%, I've got enough equity to duplicate. In most cases, while banks advertise 90-95% loans, when it comes down to the fine print, they may only go to between 50% and 80%, depending on the asset class.
2. Next, I want the high LVR *without* cross-collateralisation. That is, without having to put up another property (such as the family home) as additional security. You don't want the equity in your home to be tied up with the bank's valuation of your investment property.
3. Finally, my lender must be prepared to disclose its valuation of the property. Surprisingly, this often rules out a number of banks. By comparing the appraised value with the purchase price, I can be sure that the valuation is fair and, more importantly, that I have not paid too much for the property. The bank must also be prepared to revisit its valuation at twelve-monthly intervals, so that I can identify any unused equity.

You should be able to find a lender willing to accommodate you if you shop around, and don't be afraid to shop around – with banks, loyalty only goes one way!

What are some of the skills you've had to develop in becoming a successful property investor?

I prefer to think of it as a package of knowledge, skills and tools. I had to acquire knowledge about things like compound capital growth, market cycles and locations. I had to develop skills in identifying growth potential, negotiating effectively and so on, and I had to gather the right tools to make things happen – in particular, I needed to build a team of people who could add knowledge and skills where I was lacking!

How did I develop this package of knowledge, skills and tools? By throwing myself into the process, asking lots of questions and learning from my successes as well as my many mistakes! I'm not really an academic theorist; I've acquired my knowledge simply by doing.

What are the most important lessons you've learnt about property investing?

I guess it boils down to two pretty simple things. First, *land* is the driver of capital growth; land is what gives property its intrinsic value. Land appreciates in value; buildings depreciate in value. Buildings are a good vehicle to generate cash flow in the form of rental income and associated tax deductions, but only land generates capital growth over time. I look for at least 40% land content, that is, I look for 40% of my purchase price to represent the land value. As an accelerated wealth building strategy, I also look for the potential to subdivide or re-zone the land, which can instantly increase its value per square metre – that really kick-starts capital growth!

Second, capital growth must drive duplication, one investment property won't make anyone wealthy. Using the increasing equity in a property to acquire another property and repeating the process again and again, will. That's how you harness the power of exponential growth…growth on growth on growth. I *love* the way the maths works!

It seems that everyone has an opinion about property, how do we differentiate the good advice from the rest?

It's true, and there's 'bad faith' as well as just plain 'bad advice'. It's a shark pool out there! Mind you, I take a lot of advice from different people because it's important to keep learning and investigating –

> ❝…as an investor you also need to avoid being manipulated by the greed of others.❞

you just have to be discerning. It's a bit like food. There are all types of restaurants out there selling all types of foods – fast food, junk food, rich food, spicy food – I like healthy food, so I'm very specific about what I eat and where. There are plenty of other options, but I'm happy to ignore them.

Most of all, I look at the person giving the advice and ask myself whether this is a person with integrity. That's about more than just 'doing the right thing', it's about having discipline, truthfulness and authenticity. For me, it's also about giving advice based on direct experience, not just half-baked or second-hand ideas. I'm often asked about shares and options and I'm happy to tell people straight out that I can't advise anyone in those areas because I don't have a track record of success with them. I prefer my advisers to have at least ten years' experience in their chosen field. In property, that means they will have been through at least one downturn.

What are some of the reasons why an investor could lose money in property?

One reason is because a person has based their decisions on emotion or greed and another is not doing their homework. I reckon these two things alone catch out about 95% of punters.

Greedy investors are usually locked into 'get rich quick' thinking and they end up shooting themselves in the foot in all sorts of ways, such as making false economies, pricing themselves out of the market and selling short of real growth.

Unfortunately, as an investor you also need to avoid being manipulated by the greed of others, which is why doing your homework is so important. These are my own top six questions to ask before buying an investment property:

1. Ask yourself *why* you're buying. Is it for income? Capital growth? Or are you just sentimental about a particular house or suburb? Make sure

that you have specific financial goals which keep you on track with all of your investment decisions.
2. Check the property's land content. This is where the capital growth is.
3. Check comparable sales. Find out what other owner-occupiers have paid for adjoining properties. This is the best guide to value.
4. Check the established capital benchmark – the highest valued property in an area. I look to pay substantially less than what my neighbours have paid to get into the area. With 'the worst house in the best street', there's immediate potential for capital growth.
5. Check rental demand and vacancy rates in the area. Vacancy is income downtime. Cash is like oxygen, if you run out of it, it's all over pretty quickly!
6. Check the age of the building. Houses built after 1985 can be depreciated, making a huge difference to your cash flow.

What do you think are the most common mistakes that new investors make?

In my opinion, it's buying units. Duplexes and houses with at least 30% land content fall into the category of effective wealth-building assets. Townhouses within seven kilometres of a CBD can also sneak into this category. But say you buy a residential unit as an investment over a ten or twenty-year period, as some 34% of investors do, the proportion of land value to building value is perhaps 10:90. Land appreciates, buildings depreciate and you end up with limited capital growth (other than inflation) for the first five to ten years. I believe this is *not* the way to start building a property portfolio.

If you had to start again, with only $100,000 equity in your own home, what would you do?

I'd set myself a goal of creating $1 million in cash within one year. One year isn't a long time in property, so I'd spend the first month selecting a geographical location and identifying expanding businesses that have a

> **You really can't do anything without having the desire. In fact, it's often said that you need a burning desire.**

demand for land in that area. A prime example at the moment is childcare centres, but it could be a McDonalds drive-through or a garden centre. I would then try to supply the businesses with property suited to their needs.

Say I chose the childcare industry. I'd plot all the childcare centres in the city I was researching, identify councils with existing development applications, and match my findings with population growth areas to identify where the need will be in the next one to three years. I would then hone in on those areas, visiting councils to identify the zonings and land areas I would need.

I'd gather an 'A-Team' of expert architects, engineers, surveyors, and so on who have worked on projects for some of the larger businesses in the childcare industry. Having done the homework, I would find potential sites and contract to purchase those sites, subject to approval for a childcare centre, and ensuring that I had a clear and convincing exit strategy in place. I'd negotiate to put down a minimal deposit (maybe $5,000 per site) and submit my application to council. During the approval process, I'd endeavour to sell the sites with approvals.

I'd be looking at acquiring residential land at say, $200-250 per square metre, and on-selling it with approval for a childcare centre at about $500 per square metre. To achieve my goal of generating $1 million in cash, I'd need to obtain approval for, and on-sell, maybe four sites…it's just an idea.

One more thing about 'starting again'. As a success coach, I stand on my track record, but sometimes track records can be irrelevant because they don't say anything about our potential for the future. Understand that the past doesn't define who you are. If you haven't achieved your goals in the past, that doesn't mean you can't achieve them now. I believe in 'reinventing' oneself, a commitment to success is a commitment to constantly thinking about who we are, leaving our limitations behind and taking hold of new possibilities.

What do you think are the essential qualities of a successful property investor?

In my experience, successful wealth builders have three things in common. First, they are positive and optimistic about the future, continually looking for opportunities and ready to have a go. Second, they are responsible, ready to use what they've got and they avoid blaming others for their circumstances. And third, they're proactive – they set clear, challenging goals and go for them, decisively.

Around 75 years ago, Napoleon Hill wrote the book *Think and Grow Rich*. He said that the two biggest mistakes people make are allowing themselves to be influenced by negative people and not acting quickly enough. So many people I talk to at my workshops admit that they don't have goals, that they're caught up in the blame culture, or that they procrastinate, particularly when it comes to financial decisions. Fortunately, this can be turned around.

Goal setting seems to have been extremely important in your achievements. What does it mean to you and how do you do it?

Goal setting is *the* most important thing. As Friedrich Nietzsche said, 'He who has no goal, has no direction'. You really can't do anything without having the desire. In fact, it's often said that you need a *burning* desire. To me, having a burning desire is setting a goal and making it a priority to achieve that goal.

Here's my very simple three-step process for goal setting.

1. First, I start by identifying the goal. I ask myself if it sits well with my core values, if it's something that I believe in and will be willing to take

the time and effort to achieve. If it is, I know I'll be better able to hold onto that goal when the going gets tough.
2. Then I try to clearly visualise what achieving my goal will look, sound and feel like. I really believe that if you can't 'see' it, you won't make it happen. Tiger Woods visualises every shot he makes before he makes it and 'sees' the ball going into the hole on that last putt. Many other successful sports and business people do the same thing. I practise my visualisations often. It may be a little fuzzy at the start, but it gets clearer and clearer. That's when you begin to find that 'providence moves'. When you are tuned in to your goal it's amazing how opportunities and resources seem to come to you.
3. Finally, I take the time to consider what obstacles may be preventing me from achieving my goal and I develop plans and resources to overcome them. This contingency planning gives the rational or critical part of my brain something to chew on, as well as the creative side.

If anyone can succeed in property no matter what their current financial circumstances are, what do you think holds people back from becoming property millionaires?

So many Australians say they are 'interested' in property investment yet the ABS Census suggests that only about 3% of us retire above the poverty line. I think there are a number of issues here.

First, we hold ourselves back. There are so many motivation-killing things we tell ourselves about wealth building such as, 'I don't have enough money (or expertise)', 'debt is bad', 'wanting wealth is greedy', 'owning a home was good enough for Mum and Dad, so it should be good enough for us', or simply, 'she'll be right, there's always the savings or the pension'. None of these things are true or even need to be obstacles. Perhaps we identify a little too much with the great 'Aussie Battler'. Our culture doesn't always embrace success as a key positive value (other than in sport). I believe that success is a choice and you have to make it.

Second, being 'interested' by reading books and going to seminars isn't enough. You actually have to do something about it! It's the starting that stops most people.

And third, too many people who do 'dip a toe' in the water fall foul of the sharks or just don't go about it the right way. You have to do your homework.

Early on in your life you experienced a few setbacks. What were they and how did you turn them into opportunities?

It's funny, so many people know my story through my books and through the television program, *Australian Story*, and they often focus on the setbacks or adversity I have experienced. My father was killed in a car accident when I was eight years old. At the age of ten, I was sent away to boarding school – and the first two or three years were pretty tough, boarding school certainly makes you independent. When I finished school at seventeen, I found myself on the Gold Coast, alone and with only a knapsack and a couple of hundred dollars in my pocket. That was my opportunity to get in amongst it and learn what life was all about.

My journey hasn't been about turning setbacks into opportunities, so much as about learning from them. It may sound strange, but even at the time of my father's death I had the sense that everything happens for a reason. That set me on a path to discover my own purpose in the world, to practise awareness, to stay open to signposts and the potential value in all people. I also learnt that nothing is permanent, which helped me to develop a kind of detachment. Both of these lessons have been immensely helpful in my wealth building career.

> ❝...too many people who do 'dip a toe' in the water fall foul of the sharks or just don't go about it the right way.❞

In many ways, I had a great childhood surrounded by great people. While I never did well academically, I did excel at sport and that teaches you a lot about winning, losing and playing the game. I once read that of the top 500 CEOs in America, the majority excelled at some type of competitive sport at some time during their lives. That makes sense to me. Through sport I learnt to do what I can do, to the best of my abilities and to enjoy the journey along the way.

So, I don't really see these things as setbacks, but as opportunities to learn and define the person who I have become today.

Who are the mentors that have inspired you, and what important lessons have you learnt from them?

My first mentor was George Margolis, whom I met when I was just seventeen. George had built a fortune in real estate during the 1960s and lost it in the crash of 1974-5. He was emerging from the bottom of his rollercoaster and the timing was right for us to get together. With his knowledge and contacts, and my energy, we made a great partnership.

George taught me a lot, but I'm particularly grateful for one lesson. There's an old saying, 'Learn to like your dislikes'. George turned that into, 'Do two things every day that you don't like doing'. I was (in those days) a late riser and hated knocking on doors. George encouraged me to get up early and start knocking on doors for listings, first thing in the morning. I told myself that I wouldn't go into the office until I had one or two good new listings. After three months, it became like a game to me. I started to enjoy it and look forward to the next day's door knocking. I learnt that discipline is the key to success in any endeavour, I also learnt that feelings are no barrier to effectiveness. And along the way, I became the most successful real estate salesman in the area.

My second mentor was Michael Hershon, chairman of one of Australia's largest development companies. He taught me about people and how to be careful when choosing the people you do business with. As they say,

'You are better off shaking hands with an honest man than signing contracts with a crook'. He also taught me that it was important for me to honour my responsibilities and to do what I say I'm going to do, or better. I think that's pretty rare in property.

The amazing thing for me is that we really don't choose our mentors – they choose us. Mentors come into our lives as we get out there, making relationships and knocking on doors in search of opportunities. They identify us as someone who has the potential to walk the same path they have walked. That's been my experience.

Are there any significant quotes that you live your life by?

There's so much wisdom to draw on. One of my favourite quotes is by Goethe:

'Until one is committed, there is hesitance, the chance to draw back, always ineffectiveness. Concerning all acts of initiative and creation there is one elementary truth, the ignorance of which kills countless ideas and splendid plans; that the moment one definitely commits oneself, then providence moves too. A whole stream of events issue from the decision, raising in one's favour all manner of unforeseen incidents and meetings and material assistance, which no man could have dreamed would come his way. Whatever you can do, or dream you can, begin it now. Boldness has genius, power and magic in it.'

That's been true for me. I see wealth building as a journey. The companions and mentors, the opportunities and resources are all out there ahead of you, but you have to step out onto the path.

What does financial freedom mean to you?

I'm not really into 'toys'. My property portfolio has mainly given me *time* to do the things I want to do. For many years, I was on that financial treadmill where you have to work within a particular window of time, because time equals money. In property, it was the mortgage interest payments clicking over month after month. I'm still working 40-50 hours a week, but now I do it out of the motivation to develop my passion, rather than the need to earn more money.

For me there's also another element to financial freedom, the element of custodianship. I firmly believe that those few of us in the world who are fortunate and knowledgeable enough to create, control and enjoy wealth have a responsibility toward those who aren't and don't. We are not just wealthy individuals, we are custodians of the world's wealth in our society, and we have a purpose and responsibility that goes beyond just meeting our own needs and those of our families.

It became clear to me in 1991 that I could have retired with an annual income of $300,000 for the rest of my life. It was what I always thought I wanted, but when I got there, retiring on my wealth seemed like a huge cop-out. I still needed a challenge and a purpose. My wife and I decided to establish our own charitable foundation for youth at risk, the plight of

John with boys from his Toogoolawa school.

whom had concerned us for some time. The Toogoolawa project now consists of three unique schools, which offer education and opportunities to kids who have fallen (or been pushed) out of the mainstream school system. I started by giving money but I was soon challenged to give something more of myself. I now spend many hours every week with the Toogoolawa kids teaching outdoor education, communication classes and other activities.

There's a great quote from the Indian poet Rabindranath Tagore that I love, 'I slept and dreamt that life was joy, I awoke and saw that life was service, I acted and behold, service was joy'. That's a big part of what financial freedom means to me.

What are some of your plans or goals for the next five years?

I'm a fan of challenging goals that stretch our passion and develop our sense of purpose. Today, my goal is to expand the Toogoolawa schools program from three schools to 50 within the next ten years. There's a tremendous need, which helps to fuel the 'burning desire'. It's easy to visualise because I already have the experience of the current successful schools to go on. I picture hundreds of kids with dozens of teachers meeting at our annual combined schools get together, what a party. Now, *that* will be a success story!

INCOME VERSUS GROWTH

GORDON GREEN

> " I am seeing a lot of new investors rushing out into country areas to buy property that is barely showing a positive cash flow. This could be the biggest disaster to hit the investor market. "

PROFILE

GORDON GREEN

Gordon Green was born in 1946 in the Queensland country town of Gympie. After completing Year Ten at high school, he moved to Brisbane and began working as a clerk in a motor dealership. He completed his degree in accounting by studying at night while working at the dealership during the day.

After two years of National Service between 1967 and 1969, Gordon did a variety of different jobs before forming a business and investment consultancy firm with three partners in 1971. The firm was sold in the late 1980s and Gordon then spent two years as the state investment manager of Australia's largest building and development company. During this time, he also started a project management company which he went on to manage full-time for the next five years.

In 1997 Gordon founded Profitable Business Concepts Pty Ltd (PBC), which has grown to become a comprehensive 'one-stop investment-shop'. PBC provides a range of services to large and small investors alike, including adult training and education, real estate investment, financial planning, finance broking, property construction and development, life coaching and business acceleration coaching.

Since purchasing his first property at just seventeen years of age, Gordon has build a property portfolio worth well over $10 million and has completed more than 2,500 real estate transactions. Today he is a sought-after teacher and mentor, and attracts audiences from all over Australia and New Zealand to his workshops.

Gordon lives and works in Brisbane with his partner Janny, and outside of his investment career enjoys boating, motor racing and is a keen dancer.

Why did you decide to start investing in property?

I come from a poor family (or perhaps I should say 'economically challenged', to be politically correct), my mother struggled and at the age of 50 was still living in rental accommodation. I was determined not to end up like that. I bought my first property at the age of seventeen and have been involved in the industry ever since. I had three partners, because none of us had enough money or borrowing capacity to buy anything on our own. It was a five-bedroom house in Indooroopilly, Queensland, which we rented to uni students. We sold it after a short time for a great profit which enabled us to go on and buy our own investments.

Over the last 40 years I have had my ups and downs in real estate and those experiences have helped me formulate some solid rules and attitudes about investment.

What do you love about property?

Property can have all of the essential elements required for a great business – it has the ability to create surplus cash flow, you can add value which creates instant capital whenever needed and there is predictable long-term asset growth. Any business with these three components has a far greater chance of success than a business that just creates cash flow.

Another thing I like about property is its flexibility – I can choose the level I want to play at, how much I want to play with, whom I play with and where I play. I can operate anywhere in the world and can do as much or as little of the work as I want by employing people to do the things that I don't want to do. And one final thing, which is kind of neat, is that you don't need to know everything about property before you can make money. So if you're reading this and don't want to be a professional investor or can't be bothered learning everything there is to know, just get out there

> **When you make a lot of money quickly, you sometimes forget it may not always be that easy and you neglect to plan for the future.**

and buy something and you'll probably still end up comfortable, it's that easy. But if you do want to become seriously wealthy through property, there are a few things you need to understand. Wealth takes a little more than just luck.

What's one of the best deals you've ever done and why did it work so well?

The best deal is hard to choose, some of the most profitable deals may not be considered the best because of the effort or concerns they created. But if I had to choose the best deal ever, I think it would be the purchase of a 25-year-old, 1,000 square metre commercial property in the year 2000. A business partner and I agreed to go 50/50 in the $1.1 million purchase and financed it with a $100,000 deposit. My partner spent about $60,000 on renovations and we ended up renting half each for our respective offices.

After eighteen months my partner needed the entire space to increase the size of his operation, so we agreed that I would move out and that he would purchase my share at whatever the current valuation was. It came in at a cool $2.5 million, less my share of the debt ($350,000), which left me with a net profit of $900,000. This was *all* profit as his company and my business had paid sufficient rent to cover the interest and principal reduction. Now, most would think this was a great result but the best was yet to come.

Because my business needed another home, I purchased a newer and larger 1,100 square metre property in the same area (but in a better position) for the bargain price of $1.4 million and a delayed settlement of twelve months. This building, with about $200,000 spent on improvements, is currently valued at $2.7 million and has a debt owing of $700,000. The overall result is that my original outlay of $50,000 (half the deposit on the first building) is now worth $1.9 million in just three years. In the next five years, when the building is paid off, if the area does what I believe it will, I will have an asset of around $3.5 million producing rental of around $350,000 per annum, all for a $50,000 outlay. Now that is what I call a good deal!

Even though your background includes more than three decades in real estate, you didn't start to invest seriously until later in life, why is that?

In the early days, I only ever regarded investment as a lucrative hobby, I bought and sold and used the profits to buy expensive cars and to maintain a lifestyle that my salaried income could never have supported. When you make a lot of money quickly, you sometimes forget it may not always be that easy and you neglect to plan for the future – you spend like there's no tomorrow and if there is, you figure you'll just make more money then. Luckily, as I've gotten older it appears I've developed a little wisdom and I've realised the importance of accumulating wealth, not just generating income.

If I had to start over again, I'd still do the same things but in a different order. I would trade, develop and hold properties until I had enough income-producing assets for that income to support my lifestyle – so instead of spending all the money I created, I'd only spend the income derived from the assets I accumulated. That's what I'd do now, but it is a lesson that I had to learn the hard way.

What is your personal wealth creation strategy and why do you take this approach?

Today, my specific strategy is to create what I call 'money manors'. That is, to build self-sustaining entities that have the ability to create capital, produce cash flow and deliver high capital growth. How is this possible? Well, each money manor has at its core a business or other high income-producing asset (not a job). Around that is built a handful of positive cash flow properties which support one negatively geared property that has high capital growth. The idea is for each entity to be self-sustaining so that you get the benefit of the capital growth without the money needed to support it having to come from your own pocket. If you understand this principle, you can develop as many money manors as you like, in any market you choose.

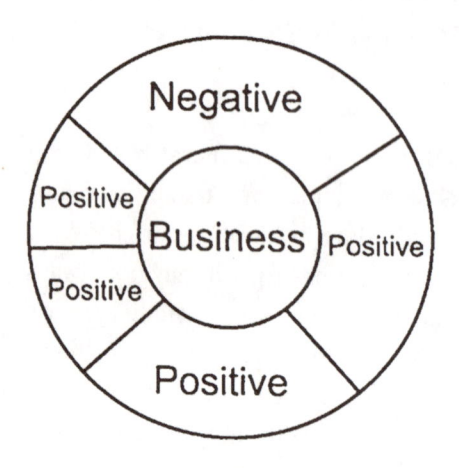

For me, property and business go hand-in-hand. Every time I want to create another money manor, I look for another business project to develop. These businesses produce the income needed for the deposits and to meet the bank's requirements for lending. The business is also there for support in times of need and to fund any renovations, which add to the overall entity's value. This business could be, and often is, a property development. If I am buying with the express intention of selling, I regard it as a business venture that must make a profit.

What do you think about positive versus negative gearing?

Both are necessary in a well balanced portfolio. The mistake I see most often is the confused investor who buys a negatively geared property for the tax benefit, instead of for the significant capital gain which is assured if you select a well-positioned property and hold onto it for the long term.

Many advisers are advocating that investors should *only* buy positively geared property. That's all well and good if you only want income, but my understanding is that income alone doesn't make you wealthy, it just provides spending money. I am seeing a lot of new investors rushing out into country areas to buy property that is barely showing a positive cash flow. This could be the biggest disaster to hit the investor market in Australia – this strong demand has put upward pressure on prices and has given investors the false impression that they are becoming rich. What most don't realise is that many of these country areas are experiencing zero or even negative population growth. With a shrinking number of paying tenants, these properties could become difficult to rent. That's okay if you have a sizeable portfolio to balance things out, but many of these people are first time buyers relying solely on the income from the property to support the repayments. I'm not saying that positively geared properties are bad, I'm just saying that you need to be well informed about demographic trends so that you can accurately assess the future stability of your investment – regardless of whether the property is positively or negatively geared.

In what ways can a property investor create a balanced portfolio?

There are three factors to consider in any investment portfolio:

1. The need for expansion capital.
2. The balance between cash flow and income requirements.
3. The need for capital gain to create real wealth.

On top of this, your portfolio must fit your personal risk profile. For example, if you have a 70% low-risk, 20% medium-risk and 10% high-risk profile, you need to constantly rebalance your asset holdings so as to not exceed these parameters. If your high-risk investment is producing great results, the hardest thing for most investors (both professional and amateur) is to reduce the amount of capital invested in the well-performing segment and rebalance the portfolio back to its original weighting. But if you don't, you'll become over-exposed to the higher risk investments and even worse, to boost profits, borrow higher and higher amounts from the lower risk areas. It's like an oversized tree with huge branches and undeveloped roots – it looks great for a while, but when a strong wind comes, the tree will fall. Through either ignorance or greed this temptation is what causes most bankruptcies – you must make sure that your portfolio is continually rebalanced so that it doesn't become overloaded with high-risk investments.

Do you recommend that people should look for properties anywhere and everywhere or just focus on three or four suburbs?

I recommend that people develop a life strategy and then a plan to achieve that lifestyle. This means at different times you will need different types of property to fulfil your requirements. If you can find what you need in three or four different suburbs, then that is the only area you would need to understand. If not, then you need to look elsewhere. If you do branch out you need to have a clear understanding of how the property market works and some carefully defined personal investment rules. With definite rules in place, decisions become easier and faster.

I believe that with the process I use, and now teach, I could go into an unfamiliar area or country and within a week be prepared to invest heavily or have determined that it is not the right area for me.

What are some of the methods you use to leverage your time when looking for investment opportunities?

I have a network of people who understand my specific requirements and I make sure that they are well rewarded for passing on relevant information to my team. I also have several full-time team members whose daily responsibility it is to inform me of developments in the market, which enables me to make the necessary decisions. Before I could afford full-time team members, I had to do most of the work myself, together with my partner and members of my family. Later, we started to employ some teenagers after school to input data and do research work, this grew into part-time telemarketers and research assistants, many of whom were university students and some of whom became full-time team members and are still with us today.

I treat my investments as a business and so should you. As such, most operations should be fully systemised which means very little time is required to train any new team members that you bring on board.

What should investors keep in mind when dealing with real estate agents?

The biggest thing is to understand exactly what you require and be definite about the outcome you want. Remember, if you're not paying the agent, someone else is. No matter what you're told, the agent has a legal obligation to act in the best interests of the 'principal' – that is the person paying their commission, so don't expect someone working for the other side to look after your interests. Either employ your own buyers' agent or become a more than competent negotiator. Also, don't expect the truth unless you are prepared to be truthful yourself. There is a saying in the real estate industry that goes, 'All buyers are liars and all vendors are benders of the truth'. This is the challenge that agents have to deal with, and at the end of the day they're also looking after their own back pockets.

Another point worth mentioning is that in a busy market agents have dozens of enquiries every day and they have no interest in ringing you back just because you want to talk to them. They are only interested in real buyers and sellers. In a quiet market, they are employed by the vendor to market the property, not to run around finding the deal of a lifetime for a casual acquaintance.

> "…if the seller feels they have been taken advantage of, the smallest request is an opportunity to get even."

What are some of your favourite negotiation techniques when buying property?

This is a whole book in itself. The most important thing is to have great communication skills. This will allow you to discover the vendor's real reason for selling and once you understand that, it becomes relatively simple to negotiate a deal that provides for his or her needs as well as your own.

Remember, you need to be in contact with the seller over the entire length of the contract, so it's imperative that they don't feel as though they've lost during the negotiation process. This is particularly important if the need arises for an extension of the contract or a change in terms. If the original deal suits the seller, further negotiations are easy, but if the seller feels they have been taken advantage of, the smallest request is an opportunity to get even. It's called human nature.

What clauses do you insert into a contract to protect yourself when purchasing?

Every contract is different depending on what I need to achieve. The clause that I most often add to the standard sales contract is one that will enable me a reasonable period of time to complete the due diligence to my satisfaction. Be wary if the seller's agent offers to insert the clauses that you require on your behalf. Remember, the agent is working for the vendor and is not qualified to write such clauses, it is the responsibility of your solicitor. I always use an experienced property law practitioner for my contracts, not just a conveyancing clerk, and I avoid using legal firms that have a large litigation practice. I'm more interested in getting correct and competent advice than arguing about it after the event.

What are your top tips for dealing with banks or mortgage companies?

1. Find a competent finance broker. If necessary, get a referral from another experienced investor, not just a friend who has bought one or two houses. When you find them, check their past performance and be cautious if a broker is giving a large percentage of their business to a particular institution.

2. Tell the bank as little as possible and don't provide more information than required. Understand the mortgage insurer is the one approving the loan, not the bank or financial institution.
3. Never allow a bank, financial institution or mortgage broker to talk you into cross-collateralisation of your assets.
4. Switch roles with your bank. The usual situation when applying for a loan is to go to a bank and beg for the money. However, each time your loan is rejected, it shows up on your credit file. A better way is to have several banks apply to *you* for the deal, in effect this is like putting your project out to 'tender'. This allows you to get a better deal and avoids having several entries on your credit file.
5. Never sign a privacy statement until the loan is approved in principle, subject to credit checks.

How do you choose a good property manager to look after your investments?

There are a number of things I look for when selecting a property manager. These are a few of my recommendations:

- Ensure that the agency has a full-time property manager who is a qualified professional.
- Enquire about the system they use for property management. Any good computer system will automatically identify payments which are in default and issue breach notices if the default is not rectified within a given timeframe.
- Look for agencies that use detailed inspection reports, not just a series of ticks on paper.
- Enquire about their vacancy rate and what they do specifically to reduce it compared to other agents in the area. In other words, what is their edge?

> **"** ...in the late seventies, I allowed other people to convince me that the market had risen too quickly and was about to implode. **"**

What is the biggest mistake you've ever made in property and what did you learn from it?

My biggest mistake was selling my properties and spending the money on things other than further property investments. As crazy as it sounds, in the late seventies, I allowed other people to convince me that the market had risen too quickly and was about to implode. I sold every property I owned (even my own home, and moved into a rental house) to free-up capital. I used the money to buy businesses that needed a capital injection to get them back on their feet: big mistake! One of those businesses cost me $476,000 in bad debts and losses over a twelve-month period, and in 1978 that was *a lot* of money. Then, I compounded my mistakes by withdrawing from investing altogether because I had lost faith in myself and my ability to make sound decisions. It wasn't until after I left my partner, ten years later (still living in rental housing), that I decided to have another go.

I understand now that it was my own internal identity that created the whole situation. I see people today who still don't understand that it's really not *what you know* about real estate or money, it's about *what you believe* you are entitled to in life.

Have there been times when you wanted to give up and what got you through?

There were times when I did give up. I quit the market for a long period of time and it took a great deal of effort from other people to get me back. I doubt that would happen again now as I have a much clearer understanding of myself and value myself and others a lot more. Now I have an unshakeable belief in myself and my team and any time it gets tough, I understand we just have to make it work. Between me and my team, I understand we can achieve anything we set out to do.

What are some of the skills you've had to develop in becoming a successful property investor?

The skills that I believe are essential for success in property investing are the same skills required for success in any other field.

Great communication skills are the start of successful investing – every time I do a deal, I am aware that I will have to communicate with that person for at least the next 30 days and will probably run into them again sometime in the future. Next, having a good understanding of finance and keeping good records is essential. This allows you to be sure of the facts for reporting and to also source appropriate finance with the right institution. You need to be able to do your research and have the patience to understand where the market is moving. You'll also need to understand the buyer and how to gain insights from demographic trends which will allow you to understand what changes should be made to a property so that it will sell or rent quickly.

If you had your time over again, what would you do differently?

I would hold more deals and sell less. Experience has taught me that real wealth comes from assets, not income. When you buy and sell you appear to be creating additional money, but what I now realise is that all you are doing is releasing your own money. Whenever I sold in the past I spent most of the money on lifestyle, which depleted my investment portfolio. Now I always make sure that I reinvest and only spend the income earned from my portfolio and not the capital itself.

> **I am challenged by much that I read because there is a lot of theory that doesn't work for the average investor.**

If you had to start again with nothing, what would you do?

Depends on what you call 'nothing'. If it was just a lack of money and I still had the knowledge that I possess today, I would find a development site and seek to raise the funds using 'Other People's Money' (OPM). One way would be to find a joint venture partner who would participate in the profit of the project, another would be to borrow the money from a handful of investors and give them a return of between 8% and 15% on their money.

If I had to start again with no money *and* no knowledge, I would buy a dozen books and go to half a dozen seminars to see how others have achieved their wealth. Next, I'd sit down and formulate a complete plan, starting with my desired retirement date and the amount of passive income required to sustain that lifestyle, and work backwards to find my starting point. Then, I'd just do it.

Who are the mentors that have inspired you, and what important lessons have you learnt from them?

I learn from everyone I meet. Specifically, when I was 23, I was fortunate enough to meet a 60-year-old bank manager named Roy, who took the trouble to teach me the basics. He gave me four rules and guaranteed to back me every time I came to him with a deal that met those requirements – and he always did. It was a funny thing but every time I broke the rules and had to go elsewhere for finance the deal didn't have the same results.

I also highly value the lessons of Jim Rohn's work, Edward DeBono, James Redfield, Wayne Dyer... the list goes on. John Burley, Jan Somers, Dolf de Roos and Robert Kiyosaki are all good for ideas although I don't agree with everything some of the real estate guys do. As a matter of fact, I am challenged by much that I read because there is a lot of theory that doesn't work for the average investor.

The most important lesson I have learnt is to listen to everyone. Then I look at how what it is they have to teach will fit into my investment portfolio and make my own decision about what I wish to achieve. If it fits, do it; if it doesn't, I file it for later.

Are there any significant quotes that you live your life by?

One of my mentors, Jim Rohn once said, 'Always work harder on yourself than you do at your job or business'. This advice has always helped me to understand where to focus and what's important.

Having now passed on your knowledge to hundreds of other people, what are a few of your most inspiring success stories?

I'm not sure if Martin in Adelaide would come first but he would have to be right up there. When he began he was some $40,000 in debt, and within two short years he had accumulated a property portfolio worth around $2.4 million and it has continued to grow from there. I don't claim that it was all my doing, as a matter of fact I believe that he was so committed he would have done it without my help, but I do think that I saved him considerable time, effort and probably money too.

Another person I'm proud of is a man from a small country town in Victoria who, after just one year, could afford to take his wife and two small children to Santa Land for Christmas. This mightn't sound like much until you realise that it was Santa Land at the North Pole – minus 27 degrees Celsius and all!

There is also my son who was able to retire in his late twenties. I think part of the reason for this was that from a young age he became very conscious about money and disciplined with his spending. For example, his criteria for purchasing second-hand cars was always based on how much registration was left; when the rego fell due he would either sell it or take it down to the wreckers and see what else he could pick up – I don't think he paid rego in ten years! His first property was an investment (he could never have afforded his own home on a first year apprentice mechanic's wage) and from that start he now lives the life he chooses. Today he can afford to pay cash for whatever he wants because the money he saved on cars and other toys was invested. He put his money to work first, and then spent the income it produced.

Then there is the young eighteen-year-old bloke, sixteen years old when he started, who is currently in England completing a round-the-world trip paid for with the money he has made from his property investing. I don't think he will ever know what it is to have an average job as he has always been a full-time property investor.

Then there is me, an incredible work in progress. A quiet, shy country kid who is striving to make a difference.

Why do you believe it is important to never stop learning?

There is always room for improvement and to never stop learning. The more I learn, the more I understand how little I understand. The market constantly changes. Sometimes people get confused about wealth, it's not always about money. I would rate knowledge and connections higher than money every time when discussing assets or wealth.

The key to learning is application. You can have all the attitude, skills, strategies and knowledge available but if you do nothing with it, it will be worth nothing.

If anyone can succeed in property no matter what their current financial circumstances are, what do you think holds people back from becoming property millionaires?

I believe that most people don't understand how easy it really is. All you have to do is work out a plan, set down some rules and go out and do it. The things that hold most people back are their upbringing and a belief that they don't deserve to be rich. As a society, we don't seem to encourage people to become the best they can be. So rather than waiting for everyone else to change, it is up to the individual to take responsibility for his or her own future and to get out there and do what they need to do to get the results they want in life.

What do you say to people who think it's too late for them to get into the market?

There's another boat coming called 'tomorrow'. Stop making excuses and do whatever is necessary to catch the next one. For some it may be necessary to adjust their reality about what they can afford. I believe most first home buyers would be better off continuing to rent and buying an investment property. This will force you to develop good money management habits by denying yourself the instant gratification of getting your dream home and having nothing else to work for. I believe that only when you have your property investment portfolio underway should you start looking for your own home. Delayed gratification is an essential message to all investors, learn to plan for the future instead of being seduced by the disease that so many of our generation have caught, called 'I want it all now'.

> **Sometimes people get confused about wealth, it's not always about money.**

When do you think is the best time for someone to start investing in property?

Now! Seriously, *now* is always the best time to buy property. *Where* often varies, *what* often varies, *why* often varies, *how* to finance it will vary but the right time is always now. Not tomorrow, now.

How do you think parents should go about educating their children to be 'financially intelligent'?

I think one of the most important things you can do as a parent is to set rules and give your children positive incentives. When each of my children turned ten, I gave them $50 a week each (a lot of money twenty years ago) and they had to develop budgets for *all* of their needs, including clothes, school fees, gifts, hobbies and so on. They could borrow from me at any time, provided that the loan was repaid with 10% interest the next week.

When they reached the age of sixteen, we stopped the pocket money and they had to get part-time jobs. This helped them to understand how to balance their social life and studies around work commitments. We took 25% of their earnings as board, so that they would understand that they needed to contribute to their own upbringing. We put that money into a separate account and made a deal with them whereby we would match their savings dollar for dollar. This meant that if they saved $5,000 toward a car, house or overseas trip, we would put in an equal amount, thus giving them $10,000. This worked really well and at no time did we have to contribute our own money to this scheme.

All of this teaching and education aside, ultimately the best thing you can do is to set a good example. When I look at my children, I see that they have done what they've seen their parents do which is not always what was best for them financially. My son, now 28, has just retired and can choose to never work again, while my daughter still has bad debts. The reason I mention this is because I believe my children have simply reflected what they saw growing up in an environment where their dad worked to earn the money and their mother spent it. This created a perception that the male had to be the provider and the female didn't need to worry about money. This was not the reality, just their perception. The reality was that I worked and their mother handled the finances.

In future, what type of property will you invest in and why?

Although I've made some great money in commercial property, I am fundamentally a residential property investor. The majority of my portfolio is made up of rentals that are in the mid to lower end of the market. I like the income derived from multiple dwellings but understand that they are not likely to create the capital growth which good quality, stand-alone housing gives. I currently keep a balance between income-producing properties and capital growth properties and still do the odd quick buy and sell to create additional capital. Most likely I will continue with these strategies as they have worked well for the last 40 years and I see no reason why they shouldn't work in the future.

One thing that I *will* have to change is the style of properties I invest in as demographics change. This will include such things as the size of land, the look of the property, number of bedrooms, floor layout and proximity to lifestyle facilities. At the end of the day, everyone needs a place to live, so although the style of property I invest in may change, for me residential is still where it's at.

INTANGIBLE REWARDS

Hans Jakobi

HANS JAKOBI

> 66 I've been rich and I've been on the bones of my pants... I always say to people, try rich and if you don't like it then it's easy to go back to poor. 99

HANS JAKOBI

Hans Jakobi was born in 1953 and grew up in the working class Sydney suburb of Bankstown. He attended the local primary school, and after three years of boarding school in the Riverina, returned to Sydney to complete his Higher School Certificate.

His first investment was a loan of $700 made to his father's business. Hans had earned the money working during school holidays and it was very nearly spent on records and bell-bottoms rather than invested! He quickly learnt to appreciate the power of compound interest and gradually built up the deposit for his first property purchase, a warehouse in Adelaide, which was soon followed by another in Perth and one in Melbourne. Since then, Hans has had more than 28 years' experience as a real estate investor and it has made him a multi-millionaire.

Today he travels the world teaching ordinary people how they can take control of their financial future by managing their money and creating wealth. Hans is the author of several books including *How To Be Rich & Happy On Your Income*, which is in its ninth reprint in Australia and has also been published throughout Southeast Asia.

He uses his books to support people in need throughout the world to achieve a better life and to learn to help themselves. He has licensed an organisation in the Philippines to publish his books and to distribute the proceeds among a number of worthy charities.

Hans has been happily married for more than 25 years and has three grown up children. He lives with his family on a country estate where he has established a permaculture farm and education centre to teach the practices of sustainable living.

Why did you decide to start investing in property?

My parents came to Australia as migrants and instilled a strong work ethic in me. My father left school at the age of fifteen and even though he had very little formal education he had a sharp business mind – as soon as he was able to scrape together a deposit he began investing in property.

We often spoke about money, the economy, politics and business around the dinner table. Until I went to high school, my father conducted his business from the backyard of our home in Bankstown, so I was surrounded by business whether I liked it or not.

There was always work to be done in the business and I was often called upon to help. As a child, I did not receive pocket money so the only way I could get any money was to work.

Like every other teenager at that time, I wanted to grow my hair long, buy bell-bottom jeans, invest in vinyl records and go to concerts – so as soon as I had built up a nest egg of a few hundred dollars, I was ready to go out and spend it! It was then that my father sat me down and explained that he needed to buy a packing machine for his business. He said that he could either borrow the money from the bank and pay it the interest, or he could borrow the money from my sister and I and pay the interest to us instead. Now let me tell you, when you're a teenager and you've worked hard all holidays and managed to scrape together a few hundred dollars, the last thing you want to do is lend it to your father. I struggled long and hard over this, but in the end my sister and I pooled our funds and loaned the money to Dad.

Over time, as our funds grew, the loans became bigger and bigger. One day, Dad told us that he was buying a business interstate and needed a warehouse. He encouraged my sister and I to buy it and he would rent it from us. I think I was at university by this stage and was working part-time. At

> **I like to keep my life simple and straightforward, with a minimum of drama, and when it comes to investing I like to do the same.**

around the same time, I read a biography on the Greek shipping tycoon, Aristotle Onassis, one of the richest men in the world. I discovered that he, like many others, had made much of his fortune through real estate investment. I also learnt that the rich have businesses and that nobody ever gets rich working for someone else. So my sister and I formed a company and became landlords. That's how I started investing in real estate.

What is your personal property investment strategy and why do you take this approach?

Nowadays my strategy is to invest primarily in cash flow positive residential properties. Even though I do also invest in commercial properties, rural real estate and shares, I think that the greatest and most secure long-term demand will be in the residential sector; people will always need somewhere to live. While commercial property can provide a greater return than residential property, it is often vacant for much longer and that can have a significant impact on the investment.

Not only that, but the face of business is changing as we move into the 21st century. These days more and more businesses are home-based and high-tech. Businesses outsource many of their requirements and therefore their needs for premises are changing. Generally, they need smaller work spaces and are less focused on manufacturing activities. It is important to be aware of the trends.

I prefer to buy established properties because I can assess the risks more accurately and they involve less time and effort on my part. I'm not big on renovations and property developments (even though I know some people do particularly well out of them) because I live on a farm far away from my chosen investment areas and the distance presents a logistical challenge for me. I like to keep my life simple and straightforward, with a minimum of drama, and when it comes to investing I like to do the same.

What does it mean to be a 'wholesale investor' and how does someone become one?

In most cases, when you buy a brand new property you pay top dollar for it and are therefore buying at retail prices. I prefer to buy more established properties where I can negotiate a better price from a motivated vendor.

I research the average price of properties in an area and make offers on properties that match my investment formula. Given that my offers are generally significantly below the asking price, I quickly find out who is interested in negotiating and who is not. Those who simply reject my offer out of hand are not motivated and so I move on. Some will accept my offer and others will make a counter offer. These are the people I negotiate with to see if we can reach agreement and conclude the sale. When I buy properties for below the average asking price, I consider myself to be buying at wholesale prices. You too can become a wholesale investor by mastering the skill of negotiation.

How do you find positive cash flow properties?

It's a matter of following a sound strategy and then *expecting* to find what you're looking for. This is something that I go into in-depth in my *Super Secrets® To Real Estate Wealth* home-study course.

A cash flow positive property, according to my definition, is one that puts money in your pocket even after the loan repayments and other holding costs have been paid. (Any tax benefits that you may enjoy from the property are an added bonus and should not be brought into the calculation to determine whether or not the property is cash flow positive.)

There are more negatively geared properties in the market that lose money for you (so you can claim a tax deduction) than there are cash flow positive properties. Some people find this frustrating and come to the incorrect conclusion that there are no cash flow positive properties out there – or if there are, they are too hard to find. This simply indicates that the person needs to invest in their education and learn *how* to find them.

Often properties may not be cash flow positive when you first see them advertised. You may need to negotiate a better buying price or think about how you can add value to the property so you can increase the rent and make it cash flow positive.

You've written a book about due diligence, what is it and what areas should investors be aware of?

Basically, due diligence is nothing more than doing your market research to the point where you feel comfortable making a decision about whether or not to go ahead with an investment.

The due diligence required varies according to the nature of the investment. When it comes to property, your due diligence work would include such things as:

- Checking the zoning of the property and surrounding area.
- Investigating council, water and sewerage rates, as well as body corporate costs.
- Reading through past minutes of the body corporate meetings to identify any major or chronic problems with the complex.
- Checking the selling price of comparable properties in the area to ensure you are not paying too much.
- Confirming the rental rates with a number of real estate agents in the area (other than the one you are dealing with).

When doing your research it is important to remember to seek independent verification of what it is you are checking out, from a source that does not have a vested interest in your investment decision.

You'll find far more information in my book, *Due Diligence Made Simple*.

What are the most important lessons you've learnt about property investing?

I have learnt three very important lessons:

1. Your tenant pays off your property for you, with very little effort on your part.
2. The rental income needs to be greater than the outgoings on your property.
3. As your property increases in value, you can buy more and more properties without saving a deposit – you simply use the equity built-up in one property to leverage into the next.

What are some of the things you've had to learn the hard way on the road to becoming a successful property investor?

I once bought a studio apartment in a high-rise building with lifts, a gymnasium and a swimming pool. While the cash flow was good, the running costs were enormous and the capital appreciation was just not there. I learnt to be more careful in my choice of properties so that I could enjoy both a good positive cash flow and strong growth in value over time.

When I moved to the country, I learnt that some of the rules that apply in the city don't necessarily apply in country towns. For example, the price differential (both in purchase price and rental return) between units and houses is much greater in the city than it is in the country. Not only that, people in the country would rather rent a cheap house with land around it on the outskirts of town, than a unit in the centre of town. This is because traffic is not a major issue in country towns – lifestyle is more important than

> **When I moved to the country, I learnt that some of the rules that apply in the city don't necessarily apply in country towns.**

> **The better you are at negotiating, the sweeter the deal you will strike.**

proximity to town and the cost of renting a house can be much the same as renting a unit.

At various times I've sold properties, and while I don't regret having done so, because I had a good reason for selling them at the time, the value of those properties has increased substantially since I sold them. Wherever possible, you're better off holding your properties and borrowing against your equity than selling.

One small tip to be careful about when using borrowings to fund your lifestyle – when you use the money for private purposes the interest is not tax deductible. The good news though is that the equity drawn down is not treated as income and is therefore tax-free. Taxation laws are constantly changing so it is best to obtain advice from a professional tax adviser before considering any course of action.

One of my favourite mottos in life is, 'Never cry over spilt milk'. I don't agonise over what I could have done better in the past. I aim to make the smartest decision I can after taking into consideration the facts I have available at the time. Once I've made my decision, I move on and don't look back. My belief is that the past is over and cannot be changed anyway; the future has not yet occurred, so the only thing that matters to me is the present moment.

What do you think are the essential qualities of a successful property investor?

The first quality is strategic thinking. Learn as much as you can about property investing and adopt a formula or strategy that will help you to achieve your goals. Make sure that you learn from someone who is actually rich, someone who 'walks their talk' and is a true independent educator. I have nothing against real estate sales people and love to do business with them, however I do object to property marketeers who pretend to be educating you when in reality all they are trying to do is influence you to purchase the properties they are selling. I am one of the few educators who does not have a vested interest in your investment decisions. I do not accept commissions or kickbacks from what I teach. My advice is that before you listen to someone, make sure you can distinguish between education and sales spiel.

The second quality is thoroughness. Do your market research or due diligence before you part with your hard-earned money. Don't just blindly believe everything you are told. Check it out to make sure it all stacks up and see whether you can find a better deal. You may find my book, *Due Diligence Made Simple* helpful in this regard. (Yes, that was an unashamed plug because I know this book will help you to avoid the sharks!) Now is the time when the rubber meets the road. This is when you need to have the courage to take action and make offers on multiple properties that are of interest to you. Some vendors will reject your offers while others will indicate that they are willing to negotiate. At this point you need to be thick-skinned and remember the saying, 'Some will, some won't, who's next?' Don't take the rejections personally and don't become emotionally involved with any property. Just focus on the deal.

This brings us to the next essential quality of a successful property investor and that is the art of negotiation. As a general rule, I have found that many wealthy people are also good negotiators. In fact, in my opinion, negotiation is the highest paid work you will ever do. Smart property investors understand that they make their money when they buy, rather than when they sell. If they buy well, they build instant equity into their purchase. The better you are at negotiating, the sweeter the deal you will strike.

As soon as you have struck a deal, consult your lawyer and get him or her to check over the contract. Make sure that all the special conditions in your favour have been included and that there is nothing detrimental in the agreement. Once again, this is where you need to have the courage and conviction to act quickly and decisively to secure the deal by paying a deposit and arranging your searches and property inspections.

There is one more quality that you need to possess and that is the ability to celebrate your success and enjoy your wealth. 'I'm up for that one!', I hear you say. Well, don't laugh, there are many rich people who are not happy and that's because they haven't mastered this particular quality.

What do you say to people who think it's too late for them to get into the market?

I've had many people say this to me over the years, and it's usually the people who have no investment properties and/or little financial education. Anyone who thinks like this needs to take a look at their belief system because they are focusing on lack or what is missing in their lives; they need to reprogram their thinking toward abundance.

My belief is that there are unlimited opportunities. I am never concerned about missing out. If I don't get a particular deal, I know it's for a reason and that there's probably a bigger and better deal around the corner.

I also know that real estate is the same as every other commodity in that it goes up as well as down, depending upon the level of supply and demand and how motivated the vendor is at the time. I have bought properties for substantially less than vendors paid for them many years earlier – so I can absolutely assure you that real estate does go down as well as up. It's something that most people won't tell you, but it's a fact!

Just remember that real estate prices move in cycles and if you've just been through a boom period, you may have to wait a few years before you can easily negotiate the type of deals you can get in a downturn or flat market.

If you think you've missed the boat, you need to invest in your education!

What advice would you give to someone who wants to be an investor, yet says they don't have the time?

I often hear this from people and I can understand where they are coming from because we all have busy lives and need to decide between competing priorities. There is a saying, 'The millionaire and the beggar have the same number of hours in a day'. So clearly it's how they choose to spend those hours that makes the difference to their fortunes. Time is the only commodity we can't stretch or grow. We all have exactly the same number of hours available to us and we need to choose how we invest that time wisely.

Anyone who wants to be a successful investor needs to make that goal a priority in his or her life and devote the time required to achieving it. Nelson Bunker Hunt, a wealthy American investor who at one stage had cornered the world silver market, was quoted as saying, 'Decide on what you want and then pay the price'.

If anyone can succeed in property no matter what their current financial circumstances are, what do you think holds people back from becoming property millionaires?

I think there are a few major areas where people fall down.

First, I have found that many people do not have a clear strategy for investment success. When they describe their portfolios to me, I can see that there is no structure or plan. What typically happens is that they see what they perceive to be an opportunity, jump in and hope for the best. While sometimes they succeed, I hear a lot of horror stories too. My philosophy is that there are many strategies that can lead you to becoming a property million-

> ❝ My philosophy is that there are many strategies that can lead you to becoming a property millionaire. ❞

aire. You need to choose one that works best with your personality, time, money, occupation and business constraints and focus on applying that strategy. I find that the people who are least successful are the ones who jump around like a kangaroo, trying many different things and mastering none.

Second, people simply don't do their research or due diligence work. I know that due diligence is not usually something that makes you money, but it can certainly save you from losing money. People often find it a pain doing the research because it takes time and effort and they would rather have everything brought to them on a silver platter. Little do they realise, when they don't do their research, they often get caught out and end up buying their properties at retail, or worse, paying far more than the properties are really worth. I also find that after people have been looking for a property for a while, they can become frustrated and just want to buy anything so they can get on with the rest of their lives. People who succumb to this attitude often end up as shark bait. On the flip side, some people are held back from achieving success through doing *too much* research. I call it 'analysis paralysis'. It's important to achieve a balance between doing good research and doing so much that you can't come to a decision. Do as much as you need to convince yourself that you are onto a good deal and then have the courage to proceed.

Perhaps the biggest single factor that holds people back, however, is a four-letter word starting with 'F'. You guessed it: fear. There are many different types of fear, the major ones I have observed are:

- Fear of borrowing money, particularly against the family home.
- Fear of making offers below the asking price.
- Fear of negotiating on price or the terms of the deal.
- Fear of missing out on a good deal.
- Fear of not finding tenants or ending up with bad tenants.

These are all perfectly valid concerns for every property investor, but in order to achieve success, you need to think about each of these issues and find ways to overcome your fears and move forward. We all have fears and doubts and fear is not necessarily a bad thing because it stops you from jumping into a situation blind and getting caught out. It's when these fears paralyse you and stop you from moving forward that you need to find ways of overcoming them.

The way I deal with each fear is to look at the risks associated with it and consider what the worse-case scenario is. I then find ways of minimising my potential losses. When I have done everything I can do to protect myself, I go ahead and trust that I have made the right decision. If it turns out that I made a poor decision, I work out what to do about it and move on.

What were some of the challenges you had to overcome on the journey to achieving your financial goals?

Like many people, I had to juggle various responsibilities such as that of being a husband, father, son, entrepreneur and investor. I'm sure many people can relate to the struggle of trying to find money for investment when the children need new clothes, you need a new car and the washing machine has just broken down. The temptation is always to take care of your investments after all your other needs have been met. There were many times when my investment plans had to wait until other more pressing needs were attended to. Nevertheless, when you keep your goals in mind and keep working toward them, you often reach them more quickly than you expect.

At times you simply have to bite off more than you can chew and then chew like crazy! There were quite a few times when I came close to going under and had to peg-back in order to survive.

Probably the biggest challenge I had to overcome was conquering my own attitudes, beliefs and fears. For me, it was making the transition from employee to entrepreneur. Unfortunately, that didn't happen quickly or easily. Because I have a professional qualification, I started my first business with the attitude that if things didn't work out, I could always go back and get a job. Since I thought that way, the universe presented me with

> **It is easier to learn the 'how-to's than to change your beliefs, so most people only work on the strategies and techniques.**

that opportunity until I came to the realisation that I was not good employee material. It took me a while to learn to think like a business owner and investor and to cut the umbilical cord to the past. Nowadays, I couldn't imagine myself as an employee; it simply doesn't enter my consciousness.

Along the journey I've had one of my properties burn down, tenants die, numerous cash flow crises and other challenges. None of them has been significant enough to take me out of the game because I always had insurance and took whatever precautions I could. Whenever challenges arise, I face them and work through them until they are resolved. The worst thing you can do is to try to ignore them in the hope that they will go away – they generally don't.

Why is psychology so important in creating wealth?

In my opinion, creating wealth is just like building a skyscraper – there are two important elements. One is the foundation, which is below ground and therefore not visible. The other is the physical structure that we see stretching high into the sky.

Even though you can't physically see it, if you build a skyscraper without a solid foundation, it will soon topple over. It's the same when you build wealth. If you don't build your fortune on a strong foundation of prosperous attitudes and beliefs, your wealth will crumble and you will attract events into your life to remind you that you need to work on your attitudes and beliefs.

The top part of the skyscraper represents the strategies, methods and techniques that you use to build your wealth. It is easier to learn the 'how-to's than to change your beliefs, so most people only work on the strategies and techniques. Then they wonder why they have trouble maintaining and increasing their wealth.

I believe it is far more important to develop prosperous attitudes and beliefs as they will attract the people and opportunities into your life that you need to create wealth. A person with a prosperous mindset feels they have enough money and that there is plenty to go around, consequently they attract more abundance into their life.

What do you see as the major investment opportunities over the next ten to twenty years?

This is probably the most important question we have dealt with so far. In my opinion, many property investors fail to stop and think about where property demand is headed, and as a result they will get burnt as the characteristics of the property market change.

I am part of the baby boom generation, which was born between 1946 and 1964. The size of this generation is huge and has had a major impact on the economy as it moves through its lifecycle. The baby boomers created baby food, disposable nappies, pop music and the concept of instant gratification. This is the generation that was responsible for the worldwide boom in real estate during the 1980s. Today, as baby boomers wake-up, they realise that it's not long before they will want to retire – they are pouring massive amounts of money into superannuation, real estate and shares. And have a guess what this does to values?

The massive amount of funds flowing into investment markets is pushing prices to record levels and creating a real estate boom, stock market boom and cashed-up super funds around the western world. Given that super funds largely invest their money in the stock market, these funds also provide extra upward pressure on stock prices.

I believe this trend will continue for a few years yet, until an increasing number of baby boomers decide to retire. At this point, they'll be calling their stockbrokers and real estate agents instructing them to convert their hard assets into cash. Just as baby boomers are pouring their money into investments at the moment, sooner or later they will want to cash in their chips.

Here's the problem though. The generation following the baby boomers is much smaller in number and far less affluent. They won't be able to soak up all the assets coming onto the market at once and thus asset values will drop dramatically. As asset values drop, the baby boomers will need to liquidate more assets to release the same amount of cash. The problem will compound as they are forced to sell assets regardless of their value to meet their escalating healthcare and retirement costs.

This is such an important and potentially risky area that I have devoted a whole DVD to this question in my *Super Secrets® To Real Estate Wealth* course.

How do you see changes in demographics affecting the types of properties people purchase?

A popular argument is that it is the land that forces the price of real estate up and that therefore houses are a better investment than units. While I agree that land is in limited supply, I believe there is a fundamental flaw in this argument as far as the future is concerned: at the end of the day there is one thing, and one thing only, that drives real estate prices – demand.

The values of generation-x and those following are very different to those of the baby boomers. To a large extent, baby boomers grew up with the mindset that they needed to get married, buy a house and start a family. Typically, baby boomers got married in their early twenties and had children soon after. Taking on a 25-year mortgage and a house in the suburbs was part of the deal. As they became more affluent, baby boomers upgraded to larger houses and took on bigger mortgages. The upgraded houses usually had larger garages, entertainment areas, swimming pools and gardens. As part of the package, the baby boomer family also grew to include three or four children, on average.

Generation-x does not have the same family and lifestyle aspirations as the baby boomers had. This generation is getting married much later and some are not overly keen to reproduce; career, travel and inner city lifestyles excite them far more. Portability and freedom are stronger values for generation-x, and the thought of being tied down to a 25-year mortgage with a house in the suburbs does not particularly appeal. Fertility rates are dropping and it's not uncommon for generation-x couples to have just one child after the age of 30, or none at all.

When it comes to their choice of housing, it is increasingly about larger living areas with a small, low-maintenance paved courtyard rather than a big backyard. Children prefer to spend their time in front of the TV or computer rather than playing outdoors. The traditional three-bedroom house with a good sized backyard is not in as much demand with today's house seekers.

My point is that before making decisions, investors need to think carefully about changing trends and how these might affect their asset values, and adjust their investment strategies accordingly.

Who are the mentors that have inspired you, and what important lessons have you learnt from them?

My father had a strong influence on me because he was a very determined and hard-working man. Even though he did not have a lot of formal education, he had a lot of business common sense. He had a good 'gut feel' for what would sell and the best path to take. He could give me

> **They won't be able to soak up all the assets coming onto the market at once and thus asset values will drop dramatically.**

> **I always say to people, try rich and if you don't like it, then it's easy to go back to poor.**

'ball-park' figures for his business much faster than I could get them out of the computer and he displayed enormous courage both in his personal and business life and always stood for what he believed to be right.

Another of my many mentors was Robert Kiyosaki. By the time my youngest daughter was born, I was going through a major personal crisis; I wasn't satisfied with my life or where I was headed. My chiropractor told me about Robert and I attended his second series of seminars in Australia, long before he became well known. He frustrated me, annoyed me, challenged me and helped me to change my thinking. Thank you Robert! Not only did I learn a lot from him, but he was also the catalyst for me to move onto my personal development path.

Following Robert, I was influenced by Wayne Dyer, Anthony Robbins, Deepak Chopra, Louise Hay, Stuart Moore, Stephen Covey, Mark Victor Hansen and Bob Proctor. In the area of real estate, I was inspired by Raymond Aaron, Barry Black, Mark O Haroldson, Alan J Falkson, Robert Allen and William Nickerson.

All of these people and many others have influenced my thinking, moulded my beliefs and helped me to expand my knowledge.

Do you believe that money can buy happiness?

No I don't, but I've heard it said that it sure can help you find it in far more interesting and pleasant places!

Happiness comes from within and money has nothing to do with how happy you are. I've met and read about some very rich people who are very unhappy and insecure. I've also met people who don't have much money and yet are very happy. Having said that, I've been rich and I've been on the bones of my pants and I'd rather be rich. I always say to people, try rich and if you don't like it, then it's easy to go back to poor.

Lack of money is a temporary condition, being poor is a state of mind. Equally, being wealthy is also a state of mind and has little to do with how much money you actually have. My experience is that when you develop and maintain a prosperous mindset, you also attract more money and opportunity into your life. I think it is far more important to develop a wealthy mindset than to try to accumulate as much money as you can.

What is your definition of financial freedom and what does it mean to you?

I like to measure financial freedom in terms of time rather than money.

One aspect of this is the amount of time that you can continue to live the lifestyle of your dreams without having to go out and earn money yourself because your assets are generating all the cash flow you require. Another aspect is having control over your own time. I consider myself to be financially free because I can choose to go to work or not. If I want to sleep in, I can. If I don't want to go to the office, I don't have to. My business continues to operate whether I am there or not and my assets continue to produce an income whether I work or not.

I hardly ever wear a watch and often I don't even know what day of the week it is. I can see what I've got scheduled on my wall planner and I generally don't make appointments before 11am (unless I am travelling) because that suits my lifestyle.

How do you achieve a balance between your desire for money, lifestyle and relationships?

This is a very important question and one that many people cannot answer successfully. The answer is simple really. You need to work out what your values are and rank them in order of importance, then give them a level of attention commensurate with their ranking. For example, in order of importance I would rank these as:

1. Relationships
2. Lifestyle
3. Money

Therefore, I'd make sure that I pay attention to the relationships I wish to maintain, such as my marriage, my relationships with my children, parents, friends, staff, customers, suppliers and others. Then I would define my lifestyle values and work at keeping them in balance and finally, I would address my financial values.

To what extent does a harmonious family life affect your financial success?

I have found that the most successful people in life have a purpose for what they do. It is far more rewarding for me to share my success with my wife and children.

I have been married for over 25 years and having a happy and stable family life is one of my personal values. I feel it supports my financial success and it also provides an opportunity for me to teach and inspire my children to become financially successful. As a family we discuss money matters, our goals and aspirations and I am grateful for the loving support of my wife and children in the achievement of our goals.

I've also discovered that a harmonious family life not only supports your financial success but also your health and wellbeing.

How did you teach your children about being money smart and to become good financial decision makers?

As a parent I recognise that each of my children is different and has different goals and dreams to my own. I've always wanted them to pursue whatever it is in life that they wish to achieve and derive pleasure from. My goal as a parent has been to instil values and beliefs in them that will support and guide them throughout their journey. I have sought to teach them through practical examples and by being a role model. Children always learn far more from what their parents *do*, than from what they *say*.

My children are grown up now and they have all had to work for their own money. They tell me that they had wonderful childhoods and enjoyed a variety of experiences that many of their peers did not, even though none of them received excess amounts of money or toys along the way. As parents, we kept them on a tight leash and they tell us that they appreciated that. We taught them how to manage their own money and how to save for the things they wanted. We explained to them the difference between good debt and bad debt and the importance of putting aside at least 10% of their income for investment purposes.

Today, each of them is at a different stage of their career and therefore their goals vary. Our two eldest children are earning good incomes and are consistently saving with a view to investing in their own property portfolio. Our youngest daughter has taken a year off and is working and saving with a view to spending most of her money on travel. That is the right goal for her at this stage in her life. In my opinion, she needs to do this now and once she is settled in what she wants to do, she will come back to saving for investment.

One of the hardest things for a parent is to give your children guidance without appearing to be telling them what to do.

> **One of the hardest things for a parent is to give your children guidance without appearing to be telling them what to do.**

We have always taught our children to be independent and that they are responsible for the decisions they make in their own lives.

To me, true love is unconditionally loving and supporting everyone in achieving their highest potential, whatever that might be.

Having made a lot of money, how do you now choose to live your life?

Many years ago I owned a waterfront property in Sydney and would have been considered successful by most standards. Even though I had great family support, at that time in my life I was the least fulfilled. For eight years I was attached to that waterfront property and it wasn't until I let it go that I learnt a very important lesson: while it's great to accumulate lots of assets, it's also important not to become too attached to them. You should define yourself by who you are and what you stand for, not by what you have. Your purpose in life needs to be about more than just accumulating 'stuff' if it is to have meaning for you. For us it involved giving up our

Hans enjoying life on the farm.

lives in the city and moving to a farm in the country. Even though we had lived our whole lives in the city, we decided one day that it was time for a change. Today, my wife and I live the lifestyle of our choice. At some time in the future it is likely that we will make further changes.

I only do what I love. I believe that life's too short to spend it doing things you don't like. Throughout my life the things that I love to do have changed, so I've changed what I have done. I regularly re-evaluate and test myself – if I am unhappy doing what I'm doing, I make changes until I find something I love to do. I have found that the happier I am doing what I'm doing, the more my bank account grows.

My wife and I plan and book the holidays that we take every three months up to twelve months in advance, which means that we always have something to look forward to and we enjoy working hard in the meantime. It also means that we are taking regular breaks to recharge our batteries and to reflect and plan our lives. We also enjoy spending an increasing amount of time and money helping others in the community.

FREE BONUS GIFT

Hans Jakobi has kindly offered a FREE BONUS GIFT valued at $49.00 to all readers of this book…

How To Climb The Money Tree – Hans Jakobi, Australia's Wealth Coach® and best-selling author, has already helped thousands of people achieve financial independence. In this special eBook, Hans will show you how to attract more money, riches and happiness into your life. Plus, he will reveal the ten must-know steps to becoming a millionaire in today's market.

Simply visit the website below and follow the directions to download direct to your Notebook or PC.

www.SecretsExposed.com.au/property_millionaires

THAT'S A WRAP

Rick Otton

RICK OTTON

> ❝ I send my 'wrapees' a huge turkey on Thanksgiving. We don't celebrate Thanksgiving here, so imagine how many people remember receiving that turkey! I also have a money-back guarantee, if you don't like the house (or the turkey) just hand it back. ❞

PROFILE

RICK OTTON

Rick Otton was born in Melbourne in 1957 and, at his suggestion, the family moved to Sydney two years later. Today Rick divides his time between two home bases – one in Sydney and the other in the USA.

He began his career selling insurance in 1978 under the guidance of body language expert and author of several books, Allan Pease. He met his wife, Jane, while in the US in 1989 and set up business in Dallas, Texas.

In the late 1980s and early 1990s the US experienced the now infamous 'Savings and Loan' crisis, it was a real estate crash of a magnitude never before seen and Rick didn't let the opportunity pass him by. At that time, properties could be purchased for as little as ten cents in the dollar, but with no bank finance available, transactions were either based on cash or creative financing alternatives. Rick bought up entire blocks of houses and apartments and along the way re-invented the concept of vendor finance.

In the late 1990s, Rick returned to Australia to set up We Buy Houses Pty Ltd, and began applying his vendor financing principles to the Australian market. His company buys houses at a discount and then offers them to qualified buyers using a range of creative vendor financing facilities. Over the past fourteen years We Buy Houses Pty Ltd has completed over 300 property transactions offering Australian buyers, sellers and investors proven and practical alternatives to the traditional ways of transacting real estate.

Rick is the founding president of the Vendor Finance Association of Australia and has been responsible for lobbying and educating government, finance and tax officials on all aspects of vendor finance.

Why did you decide to start investing in property?

I had a job I disliked so much that playing hopscotch in a minefield would have been an improvement! I read a book that said there were only five things that increase in value over time, and property was one of them, which sure beat me being out there pulling the plough. Oh, and in case property doesn't work out for you, the other four the book mentioned were rare coins, art, precious metals and shares.

What do you love about property?

It gives me and my wife the freedom to do what we like to do, when we like to do it.

What's one of the best deals you've ever done and why did it work so well?

I once bought fourteen units from a guy in California who'd bought up big for the tax deductions that President Reagan put an end to in the 1986 budget. I had to buy them all because he refused to just sell a couple. We set a date for settlement and unbeknown to him, I had arranged to sell the whole lot individually on the same day. Crazy plan, but it kind of worked. I teamed up with an agent who would find buyers for a $500 commission on each and I covered the advertising costs. As a back up plan, I organised another money partner to be on hand to bale me out if I blew it and didn't get them all sold and settled on the same day, in return I'd give him one-third of whatever I made. I ran an ad that said, 'This is the deal…I've got to sell my units fast. Don't apply if you can't settle in ten days, if you haven't got cash or if you haven't bought property before'. I'll spare you the finer details, but we got bowled over in the rush and each time a unit sold, the agent moved the 'For Sale' sign along to the next one. The whole deal was a great success.

What are the important lessons you've learnt about property investing?

Be excited and look forward to making mistakes – You know that you're going to make mistakes, so why not get them out of the way fast so you can move forward. Everyone gets burnt to a certain extent but it's unfortunate that many people never come back to benefit from the experience. It's like burning your tongue on hot pizza and deciding you'll never eat pizza again.

Money is never an obstacle – One of the biggest lessons I learnt about investing was that you don't have to have money, just the confidence of people who do. While I was living in the US, I started buying houses in packets from the government on behalf of other investors, who in return put up the money to pay for mine. As property values improved they made a heap of profit and so did I. Another time an agent called me about a great apartment for sale, but at the time I had no money, so I called a guy who wanted to learn how to do what I was doing. I suggested that the agent buy the apartment, the other guy pay to have it renovated, then the agent resell it and we split the profit three ways – my contribution was knowing what type of apartment this would work for and the outcome was win, win and win.

Know what the other person wants – When negotiating, you have to both be singing from the same song sheet before you can introduce the piano. It's essential that you understand how to deal with people and remember that they will never accept your proposition until they fully understand it. If you find out what the other person wants out of the transaction you will get what you want by default.

Be prepared to do what others won't – For many years I worked with Allan Pease who told me to be prepared to do what the other guy won't. He also said that it was rude to put your foot in the door when someone was trying to shut you out, better to put your head in instead so that you can keep on talking!

What is the biggest mistake you've ever made in property and what did you learn from it?

I don't know if you'd call this my biggest mistake but it was certainly one of the dumbest things I've done. I once bought a three-sided house because I was too lazy to walk all the way around the outside! What did I learn from that? Well, I guess when you create a system that works, don't be too cocky or lazy to follow it yourself – it comes down to practising what you preach. Having said that, sometimes we just don't learn, I'm currently driving a car that I'd never sat in before I bought it, and have to drive with my head out the window because I'm too tall. Anyone want to buy a cheap Mercedes Sports? (P.S. Don't tell my wife!)

If you had your time over again, what would you do differently?

I would have bought a heap more A-grade properties during the bust. Let me explain. During the late eighties, in the southern states of the US, there was a 'savings and loan' crisis – basically, the banking system collapsed which meant that there was no money to loan for real estate purchases, so everything dropped in value to whatever people could pay in cash. I was buying up properties like a woman with a black belt in shopping but I was buying cheap rather than best value. In hindsight, the best value would have been the A-grade properties which only dropped by 50% as opposed to the B and C-grade properties which dropped by 90%. When the market eventually corrected itself, the A-grade properties increased in value at a more rapid rate than the other property classes did, and when lending came back into the market they were better security and collateral.

Later, on 21 November 1991, the US Government decided (in all its wisdom) to have one big liquidation auction in Dallas, Texas, to get rid of all of the unsold

> 66 Our best buy was USD$600 for a two-storey, two-bedroom condo with central heating and air-conditioning. 99

home units (condos) which it had foreclosed on – the only catch was that you had to pay cash. It was an 'absolute auction' which meant no reserve prices were set. Texans had never experienced such an auction and everyone was too shy to bid – except for 'windmill arm Rick' with his pile of cash sent over from a little band of Aussie investors. Our best buy was USD$600 (yes, you read it right) for a two-storey, two-bedroom condo with central heating and air-conditioning.

What is vendor financing and 'wrapping'?

In simple terms, vendor finance can be described as seller finance; the seller finances the buyer into a property so that the buyer doesn't need the assistance of a third party lender. The buyer then makes payments directly to the seller.

There are a number of ways a seller can finance a buyer. The more traditional type of vendor financing is where the seller has no underlying debt. Here the seller has the flexibility of vendor financing either a part of the property, for example the deposit, or the entire purchase price.

One popular type of vendor financing is using a 'wrap' which is an abbreviation for a wrap around mortgage. Here the buyer has a loan with the seller. The seller in turn has a loan with their bank. The buyer makes payments to the seller who in turn makes the payments to the bank. The paperwork is by way of 'terms contracts', the same as Landcom used to move low income earners into government assisted housing. It is important to remember that wrapping is only one of a number of vendor financing techniques. Many people confuse the terms and use 'wrapping' and 'vendor financing' interchangeably.

Can you give us an example of how it works and where the money is made?

Say I buy a run-down house for $100,000. I borrow the $100,000 to purchase the house plus another $50,000 for renovations at 10% interest ($1,250 a month). After renovating, let's say that the house is now worth $225,000. By using a vendor finance wrap arrangement, I could have a buyer give me a $20,000 deposit and finance them the balance of $205,000 at 8.5% over 25 years (with principal and interest repayments of $1,650 a month). I make $20,000 upfront, approximately $400 a month positive cash flow and a further $55,000 ($205,000 less $150,000) when my buyer sells or refinances. So money is made in three ways:

1. Money is paid to you upfront.
2. Positive cash flow with each repayment.
3. Back-end profit when the buyer sells or refinances.

I could also use a different strategy where I have my buyer purchase the property for $225,000 and I finance the deposit of, say, 30%. The buyer pays me $157,500 at settlement (which pays out my loan completely and transfers title to the buyer) and I 'carry back' vendor financing for the balance of $67,500 at, say, 8.5% for 25 years. This gives me a $544 cash flow per month until such time as the buyer pays me out. In this example, as the vendor, I have paid out my mortgage and have no remaining debt on the property, but in the first example I still have a mortgage.

A little confused? That's fine. You're just stepping into the shallow end of the pool and the deep end is only scary because you can't swim yet.

Why have you chosen to make vendor financing a part of your property investment strategy?

Let's say you only have 'buy and holds'. The best buy and holds are the properties with the most potential for capital growth, but unfortunately these are nearly always negatively geared. So you either work at the coal face every day, possibly doing something you really don't enjoy (like selling sausages door-to-door, which I have done) to cover these losses or you have other property strategies in place that produce positive cash flow to balance out your portfolio and give you a little breathing space.

Even though I own negatively geared properties, I use wrap around mortgages, lease options and second mortgage carry-backs to achieve the positive cash flow necessary to cover the shortfall for living expenses and to fund my buy and holds.

What are the advantages and disadvantages of using this strategy for creating wealth?

There are a whole lot of things I could say about this strategy, but the main advantage is that it provides cash flow fast – without cash flow, nothing else can happen. I can't eat or live or develop a business on potential capital gains. With cash flow I can put properties in place to provide future capital profits and still have cash from day one. I'm a big believer in enjoying life while we have it and I think it's a shame that many people who are wealthy on paper still can't join you for a two-week trip to Cuba until they're 70.

On the flip side, the major disadvantage is that not many professionals are up to speed on the different types of vendor financing available and sometimes this means you're spending time educating others. Just today a vendor accepted my purchase offer of $250,000 with 90% payable in four weeks and the balance in twelve months with 10% interest. Their conveyancer rejected the offer, which I'd say was more out of ignorance than anything else because they didn't know how to put the paperwork together. Fortunately the agent was on the ball. But usually, unless I go out to see them and explain and create the documents, it goes into the 'too hard' basket.

With wrapping, is it a case of anywhere and everywhere, or do you target a few specific suburbs?

I choose to target one area at a time because running all over town works about as well as a chocolate teapot. Some people believe that you need to go out to country towns, but what concerns me about that is the uncertainty of values. When properties do come up outside an area that I have knowledge of, I pass them on to friends or associates in the business. I'm currently buying properties in the outer Sydney suburbs of Quakers Hill, Marayong, Rooty Hill and Oakhurst. Next year, I'll move on to somewhere else.

Some people are sceptical about the concept of wrapping, why is that?

It's due to the speed at which this type of vendor finance has gained renewed popularity and the lack of information available. Occasionally, a media outlet writes a story but the journalist rarely has time to research the facts and instead relies on information from people with a vested interest. I have to educate legal people about 'terms contracts' (contracts where title doesn't immediately pass to the purchaser) because they're not as common as they once were. The older solicitors are

> "...unless I go out to see them and explain and create the documents, it goes into the 'too hard' basket."

much more up to speed with instalment vendor finance contracts because they were a lot more common after World War II when there was a massive growth in building, but not the same growth in lending, due to a lack of savings in the banking system. At that time many builders and sellers had to finance buyers into their properties. Before the deregulation of the banking industry, vendor financing was still common when, if you can remember, you could only borrow four times the amount you had in savings in the bank, but since deregulation vendor financing has fallen out of vogue.

By using a wrap as vendor finance the buyer doesn't receive legal title until he has paid the seller for the property – understandably, this is because sellers are uncomfortable handing over their house to someone who has not yet paid for it. The concern that some people have is that the seller won't pass legal title to the purchaser when it's due. And although I hear stories of that happening, I've never had anybody provide me with a specific case of this where the buyer made their repayments as agreed.

What are some of the common problems that wrappers have to deal with?

The first problem is that wrappers need people skills. These don't come naturally to everyone, but if you want to be successful there is no time like the present to learn. The second problem is funding multiple projects at any one time. Often you can find yourself juggling multiple transactions while standing one-legged on a medicine ball whistling 'Dixie'. But then, that's all part of the rush. Third, many people use this strategy without knowing what it is they are trying to achieve – they walk in through in the entrance without knowing where the exit is. Also, wrappers need to get comfortable with making a profit. I know this sounds odd, but no one stays in business long if they can't feel comfortable about making a profit. My experience over fifteen years is that people don't mind you making a profit as long as they get what they want, and in many cases they're glad you are profitable so you'll be around if anything should come up further down the road.

Is the purchase price critical in making the deal work and how do you go about finding properties at below market value?

To answer the first part of the question: yes and no. You see, the terms of the transaction are always more important than the purchase price. For example, one of my students recently purchased a home for $360,000 with an outlay of $1 from a seller who had to get back to New Zealand. The student then marketed the home for $399,000 and received an $8,000 deposit from the new buyer who moved in. My student now makes a $1,300 monthly profit after he takes care of the original seller's mortgage payment each month. In a traditional transaction he probably could have bought the house for $330,000 cash but this way he has no loan liability, no deposit outlays and gets immediate income and ongoing cash flow. So over the medium to long term, he will make far more from the terms of the transaction than any hard-pushed discount on the purchase price.

The way to find distressed sellers is simple. If you fix computers the market knows you as the guy who fixes computers. Likewise, if you buy lots of houses, people call you when they really need to sell a house. The other way to find distressed sellers is to connect with a handful of agents who know you'll perform when the numbers add up. Agents tell me many people call themselves investors but then can't step up to the plate when the agent calls with a deal.

How do you maintain a healthy ongoing relationship between yourself and the 'wrapee'?

This is really critical because your future business is made or lost by word of mouth and how you treat people. It's not rocket science. We're now in the fortunate position where many of our buyers purchase a second house from us when they want to upgrade. One of our clients explained

> **If you find good people in the first place, your job will be a lot easier. If you stay away from the sewers you'll avoid the rats!**

> "...people will always pay more to own than to rent, so if you give a tenant the opportunity to own they will pay what they feel the opportunity is worth."

it to me this way, 'Gosh Rick, it's one piece of paper and we're in by Saturday!' Have you ever bought something at an all night convenience store? It's rarely about the price, it's about the convenience and how easy it is to get what you want, right now. So this is the big secret: give people what they want and they will keep coming back. I send my 'wrapees' a huge turkey on Thanksgiving. We don't celebrate Thanksgiving here, so imagine how many people remember receiving that turkey! I also have a money-back guarantee, if you don't like the house (or the turkey) just hand it back.

The real key to maintaining a healthy relationship is to choose normal people to do business with. If you find good people in the first place, your job will be a lot easier. If you stay away from the sewers you'll avoid the rats!

How do you protect yourself in the wrap transaction?

To start with, we don't receive any funds from clients directly, we receive them from real estate agents who pay everything and then forward the balance to us. If something doesn't get paid it's because someone didn't make a payment to the real estate agent or because the agent has skipped town. In relation to the legal title of the property, this is handled in much the same way as when leasing a car – the buyer has possession of the property and a caveat is in place to protect your interest.

A couple of other rules we use are: we won't put people into a house that they choose themselves because we can't control the process, and, we don't allow them to buy from us without a deposit. Our buyers know they have to be better qualified than just being able to raise a pulse or fog a mirror.

Our default rate has proved to be about the same as the banks'. Sourcing a good wrap buyer has become much easier as the market has become more accepting of vendor finance. And, as a result of buyers being able to own their home sooner or refinance earlier, we attract clients that are prepared to invest a little bit more to adopt our system.

We've heard that you are able to use wrapping to convert a negatively geared property into a positively geared one. Can you explain how this works?

I just finished recording an interview with a previous executive of a large computer company who bought three negatively geared properties off the plan in the Docklands area of Melbourne. He called me a few weeks ago and told me how he bought them at a seminar, only to discover later that they had been massively overvalued. I told him how he could turn things around and make them a positive cash flow investment. He was an excited and willing student so we met up and went through step-by-step exactly what to do. Just yesterday he called to say that he was over the moon because his properties had gone from $40,000 negatively geared to $30,000 positively geared – and he did it all from his office in Sydney! With his permission I recorded our conversation which described the four strategies I suggested he use. People are welcome to contact my office for a copy of what I affectionately call the 'Negative Gearing Rescue Pack'. Just remember, people will always pay more to own than to rent, so if you give a tenant the opportunity to own they will pay what they feel the opportunity is worth to them, which is usually enough to turn the repayments on a property from negative to positive.

Some people ask how I've been able to be so unorthodox and get above-average results. But you have to remember that I first started buying properties in a foreign market where vacancy was 12% not 2% and property values in some cases fell 50-90%. So what I learnt and the way I do it is just different.

Is there a limit to the number of properties you can acquire through the strategy of vendor financing?

This depends on how you fund them. Also, it's not always the best strategy to just keep on building up lots of properties, it becomes a case of the law of diminishing returns, where the overheads start eating up the extra profits. Our strategy is to only keep 36 or so properties in each city and have these constantly turning over with people refinancing and moving on. Our money lenders like it this way, we can automate the business, our cost-profit ratio works out better and we can have the lifestyle we choose. This summer I'm hiring one of those really big Winnebagos (you know the ones with the bowling alley in the back) and taking eight friends to see the Four Presidents in Dakota. Now for me, that's fun! There comes a point where you have to know when enough is enough.

Do you recommend wrapping for a novice investor and how does someone learn more about this strategy?

Yes I do recommend wrapping for a novice because once you have some basic knowledge it's hard to goof up. Even if you did everything wrong you'd still have a house to rent. In my opinion, it sure beats shares where you simply 'buy and hope'. I did that once and quickly turned $20,000 into $412. I prefer to buy and create the end result from the very beginning.

Perhaps the best way to learn more about wrapping is to team up with someone who really knows what they're doing (by that I mean someone with a minimum of five years' experience). That way you achieve 50% of the profit and obtain 100% of the experience.

Also, my educational workshops are probably the most well-known in this niche, but I don't do many because I'm usually out buying houses. I have a couple of small Masters' Groups that I meet with regularly but otherwise check out my website. The home-study courses I have are pretty good, and there are also other guys who teach what I teach in one way or another, neither is right or wrong, they're just different ways of approaching the subject. I believe you can never learn too much; I'm constantly learning when my students discover a more effective way to handle a situation.

Is wrapping the only strategy you use?

No, I use second mortgage carry-backs (another form of vendor finance) and lease options. I also buy and sell mortgages and have a number of buy and holds to for long-term growth. It's all about balance, having strong and predictable cash flow mixed with long-term capital appreciation.

We understand that you are quite a keen investor in the US, how have you been able to manage successfully investing in two countries?

I sense that the real question here is 'How easy is it for Aussies to start investing overseas?' First, let me say that most people who ask me about investing overseas have read or heard something which makes them think that they can make a fortune simply by going abroad. I don't suggest anyone does this until they have a very clear understanding of what they are trying to achieve. You need to learn about the foreign status regulations and use them to your best advantage. Sometimes this means hanging around foreign consulates for a day waiting to get the paperwork right, which can be an expensive use of your time. Seek out the right people; in my experience they usually aren't cheap, and the ones that are end up being really expensive. The bottom line is that you need to stay in these overseas locations long enough to smell the roses to really understand how the local market operates and how people think. If you base your decision on written material in a brochure then you are almost certainly going to come unstuck.

> ❝ This summer I'm hiring one of those really big Winnebagos. There comes a point where you have to know when enough is enough. ❞

> **The secret is to think outside the box and then get in, get your hands dirty and make a mess.**

When do you think is the best time for someone to start investing in property?

Yesterday! And after that, today. But seriously, the best time to buy is in a falling market when you're the only one buying and the terms you can get from sellers are much better than any discount you might get in a hot market. The prices might be higher, but it is the terms that often make the deal really profitable.

I had a couple who desperately wanted to sell but the market was devoid of buyers and although they really wanted $900,000 they agreed to $800,000. I agreed to give them their full $900,000 if they'd 'carry-back' the payments over 30 years at the rate of $2,500 per month. They agreed as long as I'd pay out the balance of $750,000 at the end of five years. Once I settled on the property, I found another buyer and I effectively became their bank. With the new deal, the buyer agreed to pay me $3,000 each month giving me a $500 surplus with a payout of $825,000 in five years, or a $75,000 profit.

You just need to throw away everything you previously knew and ask yourself what can you do to make this dog hunt? When two people come together, anything goes. When we had no financing available for houses in the US we took financing on the car and threw in the house for free! The secret is to think outside the box and then get in, get your hands dirty and make a mess.

If anyone can succeed in property no matter what their current financial circumstances are, what do you think holds people back from becoming property millionaires?

In my opinion, people don't succeed for three reasons:

1. They can't see it, so therefore they can't believe it.
2. Their back isn't up against the wall motivating them into action.
3. Their friends tell them it isn't possible.

Number three is an important one. I started out with no friends and I think that was my saving grace. I must have bought at least twenty houses from US banks before I had enough friends at dinner parties 'advising' me that banks have no houses to sell, or from what they'd heard, it doesn't work.

What advice would you give to someone who wants to get started in property investing?

When I started I really didn't know anything, and that was my greatest asset because I wasn't influenced by others who didn't know anything. Once I began doing things however, people started to give me all types of advice and suggestions, telling me what I could and couldn't do. What I learnt was that the guy sitting behind the accountant's desk doesn't hang out in European café's drinking mochas – otherwise that's what he'd be doing. So don't spend time with the 95% who aren't going anywhere. Most people take advice from losers on how to be a winner. Hang out with the right people, the ones making more than you and the ones who have a winner's mindset.

When you've experienced challenging times, what kept you going?

What keeps me going is the thought of being unemployed – the thought that if I gave up I'd have to go down to the Centrelink office and stand in those long queues and fill in those forms. I hate filling in forms. I usually tell people that I can't read or write (which works by the way, people just look at you in disbelief and offer to fill in the forms for you!).

What is one of the funniest things that has ever happened to you in your property career?

I once (by accident of course) sold a house to someone before I actually owned it. What happened was this guy really wanted to buy a house which I was still in the process of buying. From memory I told him that we were settling on a particular day and he could move in the next day. As it turned out, my settlement date got pushed back and I had so many things on my mind that I forgot to tell him that he couldn't move in. As a result of my stuff-up, he moved in and we got a very irate phone call from the vendors who had driven past their house only to find a removal truck in the driveway and a strange guy sitting in a banana chair drinking margaritas! I thought it was extremely funny, but alas I had to laugh alone.

Another time, I had an office in Dallas which was in a downstairs bedroom. I was moving a student out of one property and into another, but unfortunately the new place wasn't ready and the student had already moved everything out and into her car. She dropped by my office to let me know she really needed a place to change because she had to go out. I left her in my office to undress, and with my back turned, she passed her clothes to me to take upstairs to hang in my wardrobe. At that precise moment my wife came downstairs to be confronted with a topless teenager and me holding her clothes. From that moment the way we handled property transactions changed. Years later my wife confessed that she wasn't a bit concerned as she could never believe that a hot little uni chick could ever be interested in an old fridge magnet like me!

What are some of your plans or goals for the next five years?

When it comes to transacting real estate in Australia, I want to be recognised as the guy who asked the question, 'Why can't we do this another way?'

RENOVATE FOR PROFIT

SAM VANNUTINI

> **❝** This is without a doubt one of the biggest myths that stops investors from using a renovation strategy to maximise their real estate returns. Throughout my many years of experience, I'd go so far as to say that not having any trade skills is actually an advantage. **❞**

SAM VANNUTINI

Sam Vannutini was born in Melbourne in 1965. He is a first-generation Australian with Italian parents, and while growing up he spent most of his school holidays helping his father with his plastering business.

After a few years in the workforce, Sam became frustrated with the lack of lifestyle options his pay cheque provided, so he decided to supplement his income by becoming a part-time real estate investor.

In 1987 he purchased his first property, and as real estate values skyrocketed, he used his equity to purchase more and more properties. When the recession of the early 1990s struck, Sam found himself on the wrong end of some bad investment decisions and on the verge of bankruptcy. This experience was a critical turning point in his life. Determined not to repeat the same mistakes again, he decided that the best way to become successful in real estate was to work full-time in the industry, so he became a licensed agent.

Then in the mid-1990s Sam met a client who was looking for houses to purchase, renovate and sell for profit. Amazed by the results, Sam asked his client how he did it – 'buy low, renovate quickly, and sell high' was the response and it became the formula for Sam's success. Over the past ten years he has renovated and sold more than twenty properties and built up a substantial portfolio.

In 2001, Sam founded Renovated For Profit, a training company designed to teach people what to do (and not do), and how to make money through renovation. Sam is now an internationally published author of two books and has developed a home-study course.

At the time of writing, Sam has just turned 40 and retired from full-time employment. He now divides his time between his renovation projects, mentoring his private clients, hanging out with his wife and watching his son grow up.

What is your personal property investment strategy and why do you take this approach?

My property investment strategy is to only buy where I can add value through renovating. More recently I have also started to invest in commercial properties for the higher rental returns, which provides surplus cash. However, my main investment strategy has always been to renovate residential properties.

Unlike many real estate investors, I don't feel the need to hold a large property portfolio. Frankly, I am a bit lazy and am not a big fan of carrying a large amount of debt. I would much rather have five properties fully paid off sooner with each providing me with a 5-6% rental return, than have fifteen rental properties that will take twenty to 25 years to pay off before I see the benefits of the rental income. While it is definitely better in the long term to hold properties and take advantage of the capital growth, I don't believe that you must wait until you are 60 or 65 years old before you can retire.

What I do is sell four out of every five properties I purchase. The money I make from the ones I sell allows me to reduce the debt on my 'buy and holds' much quicker. By doing so, I create a passive income stream because my interest repayments are minimised.

What are the benefits of renovating as opposed to the traditional 'buy and hold' method?

The first and most exciting benefit of renovating is that you can fast-track your capital growth. This fact holds true in almost any market and, if executed correctly, can yield an instant 10-40% capital gain. Depending on at which stage of the property cycle you purchase, these gains would otherwise take somewhere between two and five years to eventuate, as opposed to only a couple of months of renovating.

> **Any renovation that has the effect of a buyer saying 'wow' when they pull up outside the property or walk through the front door is a success.**

The second major advantage of renovating is that you can adopt a 'quick cash' approach. So for example, if you are in a situation where you have insufficient capital to expand your portfolio, you can renovate, sell and then use the profit to buy more properties. It is also worth noting that in a rising market this strategy is twice as effective – not only do you create instant value through the renovation, but you also benefit from any capital increase as a result of market forces. If your objective is to buy, renovate and sell, I see no reason why a six-figure annual income would be out of the question. When you think about it, all it takes is four transactions per year at $25,000 profit each. Do it correctly and you can sack your boss once and for all!

The third advantage is that renovating allows you to increase your rental returns should you decide to hold onto the property. For example, an unrenovated home may rent for $300 per week, whereas the same home may rent for $400 per week after renovation. This increased rental return allows you to reduce your debt faster, or to service more debt if that's what you choose.

Which renovations do you find give you the biggest 'bang for your buck'?

Experience has taught me that buyers (especially home buyers) make purchase decisions based more on emotion than on logic. So it follows that the best renovations are the ones that appeal to people's emotions. I call it the 'wow' factor. Any renovation that has the effect of a buyer saying 'wow' when they pull up outside the property or walk through the front door is a success.

Some external improvements that can give you the 'wow' factor include a picket fence, lush green grass, clearly defined garden beds and an attractive paint job. Internally, I always have all the rooms repainted in a neutral colour and I've found that timber floors can give you one of the biggest 'bangs for your buck'. Other things that can create a stylish look without being too expensive are window furnishings, light fittings, door handles and electrical switches. I have deliberately left talking about kitchens and bathrooms until last – these two rooms are very expensive to renovate. They are important, but the secret to successful renovating is to limit your spending while creating the biggest noticeable improvements that you can. Given a choice, I think most people would prefer a fully renovated house with all of the above, rather than a crumby house falling down around you with a completely new kitchen and bathroom. Another thing that can add a lot of value is converting one large room into two smaller rooms. One example of where I did this was with a property that had a garage under the main roofline. I converted it into a rumpus room and study, which increased both the rental return and the value of the home significantly.

Do you recommend sticking to a certain number of suburbs, or is it a case of anywhere and everywhere?

Ultimately, where we purchase will be determined by how much we can afford to pay. Once you have established this fact, your next task is to look for suburbs within your price range that provide buying opportunities. Essentially though, if you can afford it and if there is profit in the deal, it doesn't really matter where you buy and you don't necessarily have to restrict yourself to capital cities, carefully selected regional centres can also offer great opportunities.

Some areas to avoid include suburbs where people don't look after their homes, or where there's a lot of graffiti and a high rate of crime. Generally people live in these areas not because they want to, but because they have to, and while there may be a large number of potential properties to renovate you'll find that there is no end market.

At the opposite end of the scale are the very expensive neighbourhoods. These should also be avoided because of the risk factors involved. People will pay a premium to live in these areas, which makes buying at a good price very difficult. However, if you do find a killer deal after doing your research, then go for it!

The safest thing to do is to look at the lower end of middle-class areas which have well maintained homes. These markets generally experience higher turnover so there is always demand, especially from first home buyers or young growing families.

When finding properties to renovate, is it as simple as looking for 'the worst house in the best street'?

The short answer to this question is no. Obviously, if your objective is to hold most properties for the long term then position is important, but you don't necessarily want the 'best' street. The reason I say this is because premium streets attract premium buyers who are prepared to pay whatever it takes to purchase in that street. Therefore you are competing against emotional buyers, which makes the task of purchasing at the right price extremely difficult.

What I tend to do is look for areas where owner-occupiers are renovating their homes. This is a sure sign that the neighbourhood is up-and-coming and provides you with better buying opportunities.

Can you give us a few examples of your most successful renovation projects?

The first example I'd like to share is a simple one. Back in the early 1990s I purchased a home on a corner block for $105,000. I sold the backyard to a developer for $35,000 and renovated the house (actually, it was more of a cosmetic make-over) for about $6,000. I later sold the house (minus the backyard) for $115,000.

RENOVATE FOR PROFIT 153

BEFORE

AFTER

> **If you know what your profit is going to be upfront, you'll virtually remove all the risk from the deal.**

Another example, which is one of my favourites, is an apartment that I renovated in three weeks in an effort to tackle the market immediately. I purchased it for $215,000 and it cost me $10,000 to complete a thorough renovation, which included a new kitchen and bathroom. All up the property cost me $245,000 including interest, renovation expenses and buying and selling costs. Within a relatively short period of time I sold it for $268,000, giving me a quick profit of $23,000. The interesting thing about this example is that my initial out-of-pocket expenses were about $30,000 because I was using the bank's money to fund the project – this meant that the actual return on my money was 86%.

Is research necessary and what type of research are we talking about?

Absolutely! Research is without doubt the backbone of successful investing. While this may appear logical to many readers, I am constantly amazed by how many people decide to invest in real estate without correct and thorough investigation. Extensive and methodical research enables you to make accurate and informed decisions. Without it, you are taking unnecessary risks and simply inviting trouble.

The parameters of your research should not be limited to the property itself. You need to know the market in your chosen area so that you can easily distinguish between a great opportunity and a poor one. Also, make sure that you know how much you will be able to sell your renovated property for. As a renovator, your research should also extend to all aspects of your decision making. So, for example, you need to research what financing options are available to you, the costs involved in renovations and the availability of tradespeople.

What makes a property good for a renovation project?

Essentially, a good house to renovate is one that no one else wants – these are houses that are run-down and require some special attention. Depending on the current market, you may need to look at properties that only require cosmetic renovations, such as painting and landscaping, as opposed to those that require more comprehensive treatments, such as replastering and new kitchens.

My only word of warning is that you should never purchase properties that have structural defects, contain asbestos or have tested positive to termite problems. The idea is to complete the renovation as quickly and inexpensively as possible – you don't want to have to deal with these types of headaches.

Is the purchase price critical in renovation projects, and how do you go about finding properties below market value?

If you take nothing else away from reading this book, understand this one principle: you make your profit when and how you buy. Any profit you make from the renovation is just icing on the cake.

If you know what your profit is going to be upfront, you'll virtually remove all the risk from the deal. The reason for this is that if you purchase correctly, at the right price, you'll know how much you can spend on the renovation without risking your profit margin.

Here's a quick example that demonstrates how important the purchase price is. Let's say that I know that a renovated property in a particular area could sell for $400,000. I'd then work backwards, deducting all of the costs and my desired profit margin. My general rule of thumb is that all costs (including interest) and profit should be about 30% of the end value, so in this example, I would pay no more than $280,000 for the property. Here's why: on top of the $280,000 we add all the purchase costs, around $14,000; the renovation costs at about $50,000; plus interest of approximately

$10,000, which means that the property owes $354,000, leaving a profit of about $40,000. If we purchased the property for $300,000, then our profit would be reduced by 50% to $20,000. As you can see, determining exactly how much you can pay for a property before you make an offer is critical to the success of the project.

What are the most common mistakes people make when getting started and how can you avoid them?

First, many people make the mistake of jumping into the deep end without considering the cash flow side of the business. Trading property is nothing like trading shares – it can take anywhere from three to eight months before you see any money, meanwhile, the bills keep rolling in. The easiest way around this is to have what I call a 'war chest' of emergency funds. This is where the strategy of selling your first two or three renovations will help.

The second big mistake people make when starting out is that they try to do all of the work themselves in an effort to save money. But in the long term this can prove to be a false economy. For example, if you are earning $50 per hour it would be silly to do a job that you can employ someone else to do for $25 per hour. The other problem is that we are generally not experts at home renovating (except if you are a builder or tradesperson) and as a result any error in workmanship will cost you big-time when you sell the home.

Putting good financial sense aside, you need to ask yourself if you really want to spend your precious spare time landscaping gardens and patching holes in walls. Obviously, if renovating is something that you really enjoy, then go for it. But most people start out while still working full-time, and between work, family commitments and the need to sleep – there aren't many spare minutes left in the day. This can lead to undue stress on yourself and on your relationships.

Finally, the lack of an exit strategy is another big mistake that many investors make. Despite people's best intentions and meticulous research, for a whole host of reasons, sometimes the property simply may not sell. If you're prepared for this and have factored it into your overall investment strategy, you'll be fine. So the key is to never buy into a project if you can't afford any unforeseen delays or hidden costs.

Do you need to have a trade or a certain skill to make money out of renovating?

Absolutely not! This is without doubt one of the biggest myths that stops investors from using a renovation strategy to maximise their real estate returns. Throughout my many years of experience, I'd go so far as to say that not having any trade skills is actually an advantage. Why? My view is that to be successful your objective is to be a project manager, not a hands-on renovator. It's easy to find a tradesperson, what's difficult is finding profit-making deals, so your time is much better spent out there in the market looking for opportunities.

How do you decide whether to do-it-yourself or use a professional?

My advice to readers who enjoy renovating and would like to do the work themselves is simple: do what you do best and let the experts do the rest.

If you really do want to tackle the renovation yourself, I suggest you limit yourself to cleaning, landscaping, painting, removing old fixtures and minor kitchen and bathroom upgrades. Work such as new kitchens and bathrooms, electrical repairs, plumbing repairs and heating/cooling systems should be left to qualified experts.

> **❝ It's easy to find a tradesperson, what's difficult is finding profit-making deals. ❞**

> **Once you have experience and sufficient capital behind you, I see no reason why you cannot tackle several projects at the same time.**

How do you negotiate the best price for tradespeople so they don't eat up all of your profits?

Unfortunately, it is difficult to negotiate the best price for tradespeople. But if you've allowed for these costs in the purchase price, then it shouldn't chew into your target profit and there's nothing to worry about. This is not to say that you should just accept any price – it's always best to obtain two or three written quotes. Alternatively, you could use a tradesperson who has been referred to you, but even then I would still recommend that you get an alternative quote. Remember, there is always a trade-off between price and the quality of work – you get what you pay for.

One way that you can get great savings is to source as many of the materials as you can yourself. The reason for this is that unless materials have already been built into the tradesperson's quote, they will either add their own margin on top of the supplies they buy on your behalf or they will just accept any price because they have no vested interest in getting the best possible deal.

Do you recommend doing only one project at a time or having a few going on at once?

When starting out, I strongly advise doing only one project at a time. It will give you an excellent learning experience and help you to gain valuable knowledge as to what is required to make it in the renovation business. Once you have experience and sufficient capital behind you to manage your cash flow, I see no reason why you cannot tackle several projects at the same time.

What are your criteria for deciding when to hold and when to sell?

My decision to sell or hold is based on various factors. The first of these is cash flow. Can I afford to hold the property? If the answer is 'yes', then the next question I ask is whether the property is located in an area which has a good history of capital growth and is therefore likely to increase in value over the next ten years. Another major consideration is whether there is a good cash profit in selling now. For example, if someone makes me an offer too good to refuse, then I'm happy to sell. On the other hand, if the market is booming, I might consider holding the property for a year or so. Once again, it comes back to your own personal objectives.

Is it possible to make a full-time career out of the renovation business?

Frankly, I can't see why not. If you take all the previous advice into consideration, I see no reason why a person can't make a full-time career out of the renovation business, just as I have. Once again, it is important to remember that unless you have sufficient capital behind you (I'd recommend one year's living expenses) then I suggest that you begin part-time. If you find that renovating is something that you enjoy, then by all means progress to full-time.

What do you mean when you say you need a 'game plan'?

When I refer to a 'game plan', think of it as more of a business plan. The amount of focus and detail that you put into that business plan is going to be reflected by how much money you want to make. Are you hoping to just make a couple of extra thousand dollars to pay the kids' school fees, or do you want to achieve absolute financial freedom where you have half a million dollars coming in every year regardless of whether you work or not?

A good business plan, or game plan, will provide you with a roadmap to follow. It will keep you on course during stormy weather and will be your step-by-step guide to overcoming challenges. Without it, the chance of you quitting at the first obstacle is high.

When designing your game plan these are just a few of the questions you should ask yourself:

- When do you want to retire?
- How much money are you going to need to support your desired lifestyle?
- How many properties will you need to own to give you that income?
- What type of properties will you need to own?
- What level of debt are you comfortable with?
- How many renovations do you wish to complete each year?
- Who are the people that you are going to need on your support team and how are you going to find them?
- What are your criteria for deciding which properties you are going to keep and which you are going to sell?

If you can answer these simple questions honestly, chances are that you will establish a game plan that is realistically achievable and not 'pie in the sky'. It stands to reason that if the plan is achievable then you are more likely to follow through and achieve success instead of becoming frustrated and giving up because it's all too hard.

What are the most important lessons you've learnt about property investing?

First, when you are investing in real estate (or in anything else for that matter), you are in fact running a business. So just as with any business, you need a detailed business plan. The reason I say this is because in business things can and will go wrong, and business plans help to foresee and overcome these setbacks. It's the same with investing, so a business-like approach must be taken.

The second most important thing that I've learnt about property investing is the importance of cash flow. In business, cash flow is the oxygen that allows it to breathe and without it your business will quickly die. As I learnt many years ago, there's no point in owning twenty rental properties if you cannot afford to hold them and make the loan repayments on time.

The third and most important thing that I have learnt is that you make your profit when you buy – so always purchase real estate below market value.

In the early 1990s you were broke, what was the biggest lesson you learnt from that experience and what made you get 'back on your bike'?

It's difficult to say that there was just one big lesson that I learnt, I learnt many things – some were related to real estate and others were what I'd call life lessons. If I had to sum it up, it would be that you need to sit down and think about where you want to go in life, and then draw up a detailed plan that will get you there. On the human side of things, I learnt the valuable lesson of not being greedy, which in all honesty I was, it led me to make irrational investment decisions and they quickly backfired on me.

Despite the setbacks though, I never lost sight of my dream of becoming wealthy. I was fortunate enough to have good friends and mentors around me who were very blunt with me in their opinion of what went wrong and how it could be fixed. These were some serious soul-searching days for me. It was the first time in my life that I was taught to sit down and think about what I wanted from life.

> **❝ Despite the setbacks though, I never lost sight of my dream of becoming wealthy. ❞**

What it boils down to is that we have choices in life. I had a choice: I could either blame everyone else for what went wrong, or I could have a good look at myself and accept responsibility for my actions. The bottom line is that no matter how difficult your circumstances are, if you clearly define what you want and make a commitment to getting it, there is nothing in life that you cannot overcome.

If anyone can succeed in property no matter what their current financial circumstances are, what do you think holds people back from becoming property millionaires?

I truly believe that creating wealth through real estate is one of the easiest things you can do. Let's face it, all you need to do is buy a house in a reasonable location at the age of twenty, do nothing for another 30 years and you'll be a millionaire.

I think that the main things that hold people back from succeeding are fear, a lack of clear and precise goals and an unwillingness to pay the price. Of all these reasons, fear can be overcome through education and goals are simple to set. However, through my mentoring sessions and seminars I have found that many people are simply not prepared to put in the hard work required to achieve success. So ask yourself whether you are prepared to pay the price now to see the benefits in the future.

Are there any significant quotes that you live your life by?

One of my favourites is by Conrad Hilton who was the founding father of Hilton Hotels: 'Achievement seems to be connected with action. Successful men and women keep moving. They make mistakes, but they don't quit'.

You donate 10% of your sales proceeds to charity. Why do you think it is important to 'give back'?

Back when things were tough and I had my back to the wall, I soon discovered who my friends were. Surprisingly, not all the help I received came from friends, some came from complete strangers who had nothing to gain from their support and this is something that I have never forgotten.

I've learnt a fundamental law of the universe, the principle of giving. If you want to be successful you must give and give first. I'm not just talking about money either, you always have something to give, whether it is a smile, a compliment or a helping hand. In the words of Zig Ziglar, 'In order to get what you want in life you must first help others get what they want'.

I have made it my business to help others whenever possible. My way of doing this has been through establishing a hands-on mentoring program to help other people avoid making the same mistakes that I made, and I also donate a fixed percentage of my profits to charities which are specifically focused on helping young people in a positive and constructive way. The future of this country is reliant on the thinking and character of today's youth. So the more help we can give them, the better off we'll all be.

FREE BONUS GIFT

Sam Vannutini has kindly offered a FREE BONUS GIFT valued at $25.00 to all readers of this book…

7 Rules of Renovating for BIG Profits – In this special report, you'll learn how to renovate a property quickly, easily and cheaply, and sell it for top dollar…or use the equity to fund your next deal. Plus, you'll learn the 8 Deadliest Renovation Mistakes most people make, and how to avoid them.

Simply visit the website below and follow the directions to download direct to your Notebook or PC.

www.SecretsExposed.com.au/property_millionaires

TAX MATTERS

Edward Chan

ED CHAN

> 66 I once calculated that a person who incorrectly structures their property portfolio could pay an extra $430,000 in tax over a twenty-year period on just a couple of properties...It's simply too expensive to get it wrong. 99

ED CHAN

Edward (Ed) Chan was born in PNG in 1959. He completed his secondary and tertiary education in Sydney before becoming a Certified Practising Accountant. He began his career in the early 1980s working with PKF International, and in 1990 he left to begin his own practice.

Today Ed is the principal of Chan & Naylor Business and Tax Accountants, which is recognised within the profession as being one of Australia's leading accountancy firms. It specialises in small businesses, self-managed superannuation funds and structuring property investments.

Ed is a seasoned and passionate property investor and developer. His unique understanding of the relationship between property investment and tax makes him one of the few accountants in Australia who truly understand how to structure property investments to minimise tax and maximise asset protection.

He is a regular presenter at property investment and professional seminars held by the Institute of Chartered Accountants in Australia, the National Institute of Accountants and the Australian Society of Certified Practising Accountants; he is also a regular keynote speaker at the National Directors' Conference of the Australian Taxation Office.

Ed has had a profound impact on the way the entire accountancy profession operates, through the development of compliance systems and practices. He is a director of Business Intranet Systems Pty Ltd, which has a membership of over 520 accountancy firms around Australia that subscribe to the company's unique system of operations. He is also a regular presenter on best-practice methodologies to over 4,000 Accountants in Public Practice around Australia.

Ed lives with his wife and three children in Turramurra, Sydney.

Being a successful property investor, why do you choose to still work as a practising accountant?

Quite simply, I enjoy what I do. Having built up a substantial portfolio I no longer need to work, so it's a matter of working because I want to, not because I have to. As a result, I can now be very fussy about the clients I choose to take on. I find it extremely rewarding to help those who want to be helped and who appreciate my input and advice. I do not consider what I do as work. It's rewarding and extremely stimulating and to be honest, I would do it for free (but don't tell my clients I said that!).

Would you say that the majority of accountants are not well informed when it comes to effective tax minimisation for property investors?

Yes, in my experience the vast majority of accountants are uninformed when it comes to effective tax structuring for property investment. I have new clients that come to me on a daily basis from other accountants who have been set up incorrectly and it costs thousands of dollars to fix the problems.

Take the example of Tony and Sue who are looking to buy an investment property. Tony works as an engineer while Sue stays at home to care for the family. As the main breadwinner, Tony is at the highest marginal tax rate and pays a lot of tax. Their accountant, who does not specialise in property, advises them to purchase the investment property in Tony's name, with the intention of achieving the highest possible tax refund for Tony. The problem with this advice is that the accountant has only taken short-term income tax into consideration – there are several other relevant taxes, all of which should be considered.

Several years later, when their first investment becomes positively geared, Tony and Sue go straight back to paying income tax at the highest marginal rate, because the property is in Tony's name. To put out this fire, the accountant advises Tony and Sue to purchase another negatively geared property to try and keep Tony's income tax at bay. This process is repeated until the accountant remembers land tax, which is by now costing Tony a small fortune. In a last ditch attempt to save the day, the accountant comes up with the idea of splitting the rental income between Tony and Sue in order to minimise taxes, but the only way that they can take advantage of income splitting is to transfer half of the ownership into Sue's name, which attracts sizeable capital gains tax and stamp duty.

This scenario has created a tax nightmare for Tony and Sue. The original advice to purchase the property in the name of the highest tax payer was based on the short-term income tax implications, with no consideration for other taxes over the long term (I'm not saying that there's never an appropriate time to purchase a negatively geared property in the name of the highest income earner, I am saying that the appropriate ownership structure should be considered carefully before you leap). If Tony and Sue had received the right advice from the beginning, they would have learnt about ways of legitimately minimising these other taxes, through more effective means.

I am constantly amazed by the number of people who buy property without the benefit of the correct advice upfront, and invariably, it ends up costing tens of thousands of dollars in capital gains tax and stamp duty to restructure the whole thing.

In your opinion, when is negative gearing an appropriate strategy?

Negative gearing is right for the right person, in the right circumstances. The traditional argument in favour of negative gearing is that a property with strong capital growth is preferable to one with a high rental return for people who already have a high income. This is because earning income (in the form of a positive rental return) attracts income tax immediately and if you are already a high income person, earning more simply means losing half of it in tax. On the other hand, the capital gains tax on a negatively geared property is deferred until the property is sold.

Where I would advise against negative gearing is when a person is on a low income and paying little tax. For this person, positive gearing with smaller capital growth, is a much better strategy. This person needs to increase their savings as quickly as possible so that they have a greater amount of money compounding away for them.

How should you calculate how much debt you can afford?

The easiest way to do this is to ask the bank how much they are prepared to lend you. The banks are traditionally conservative in this assessment and do not take into account the tax refund that you may get through depreciation. If the bank agrees to lend you, say, $400,000 then you know you can afford around $500,000, because if they took into account the depreciation effect that could fund an additional $100,000.

On the flip side, just because a bank will lend you the money, doesn't mean that you can afford it. What if in six months you find out that you are having a child, or if there is a sudden increase in interest rates or if a couple of your properties fall vacant? Do you have a strong enough cash flow to support these blows? You should only borrow as much as *you* think you can afford, not what the *bank* thinks you can afford.

Should investors pay off the principal of a loan, or stick with interest only?

Whether you choose an interest only loan or an interest and principal loan depends on how aggressive you are with your borrowing. There is nothing wrong with

> ❝...just because a bank will lend you the money, doesn't mean that you can afford it.❞

paying off the principal, but it's simply a forced savings strategy and a slow way to create wealth.

If you are slightly more aggressive, you would want to get your asset base as wide as possible, as soon as possible – hence you would choose an interest only loan. By paying the minimum to the bank in the form of an interest only loan, it means that you have extra cash flow to service additional loans. For example, if you own $1 million in property, compared with $500,000, and the market goes up by 10% you will make $100,000 instead of $50,000, which is a 100% increase. This is the power of gearing. It is simply a matter of getting your asset base as wide as possible so that you can take full advantage of any rise in the market.

Do fluctuations in interest rates concern you?

Yes. So fixing the interest rate on a part of the loan is a good strategy. Depending on market conditions you might fix, say, 50% of the loan and leave the balance on a variable rate. This allows you to balance out your risks.

What have you found to be the biggest tax or accounting mistakes that property investors make?

I am amazed by the mistakes that people make and how much money it can cost them – often hundreds of thousands of dollars. The problem is that most people's only experience of buying property is the purchase of their family home, which is generally not taxable and therefore whose name it is bought in is not usually an issue. An investment property, however, attracts several different types of taxes, all of which must be considered at the time of purchase, these include:

- Capital Gains Tax (CGT)
- Income Tax (both short and long term)
- Stamp Duty
- Land Tax

- Possibly GST and Vendor's Duty, depending on type of property and its location

If your portfolio is not structured appropriately at the outset it can make a substantial difference over time. I once calculated that a person who incorrectly structures their property portfolio could pay an extra $430,000 in tax over a twenty-year period on just a couple of properties, and the more properties someone has, the more they stand to lose. Scary, huh?

Many people purchase property without taking any advice before they exchange contracts and to move property ownership around after purchase will incur CGT and stamp duty. It's simply too expensive to get it wrong. As the saying goes, 'An ounce of prevention is much better than a pound of cure'.

Do you recommend that people purchase investment properties in their own names or through other structures such as a 'Pty Ltd' company?

The answer is not as simple as saying that one or the other is the correct way to go, it depends on your current financial circumstances. There are a lot of variables, and asking questions such as these can help you to make the right decision:

- What are your long-term financial goals?
- Are you married or single?
- Are you employed or self-employed?
- Do you own your primary residence?
- How much do you earn per year?
- Are you an Australian citizen?
- Do you have children?
- How many properties do you currently own?

For every financial structure there are advantages and disadvantages. For example, a company is not entitled to the 50% capital gains tax discount, whereas individuals are. So if the property is owned and sold by a company, the CGT must be paid at the company tax rate of 30% and individual shareholders are entitled to a franking credit on the tax the company pays. This means that any tax paid by the company can be recouped at the time of the dividend payment. Confused? Don't worry, that's what your accountant is for. The main point is that there is no 'one size fits all' answer to this question, it must be carefully considered on a case-by-case basis.

Can you make your primary residence a tax deduction?

Yes you can, by holding it in a trust and paying rent to the trust. However, I would advise against this in many cases for a number of reasons. First, the house is no longer classed as your 'principal place of residence' which means that CGT and land tax come into play. Second, given that rent is paid using after-tax dollars, it would deplete the benefit gained from claiming the interest as a tax deduction. Having said that, there are other options. For example, when you own your own home and want to purchase a new home and keep the old one as a rental, some clever things can be done with trusts to save tax. This is a great strategy but again one that must be assessed on a case-by-case basis.

Why would someone consider investing in property through a self-managed superannuation fund?

From a tax perspective, a self-managed super fund is absolutely the best structure to accumulate your assets within. Self-managed super funds typically only pay 15% on income and capital gains earned within the fund. And when a member of the fund retires, the tax rate is nil. Effectively you could earn $100,000 per year in rental income tax-free if the property is owned within the fund. Compare that to the tax payable on $100,000 rental income if the property is held in your own name. For example, one of my clients owned around $6 million in property. I reduced the tax she was paying on her rental income from $60,000 a year to $2,000 a year by transferring the properties, as an un-deducted contribution, into a self-managed super fund and had the super fund buy units in a unit trust which purchased the property from her. The result was that the *super fund* was now earning the rental income and from those funds paying her an allocated pension. Obviously there were other considerations such as stamp duty and CGT which we were able to avoid through other strategies. It should be remembered that holding assets in a super fund restricts your ability to borrow money and hence your ability to increase your wealth is restricted.

There are a lot of rules associated with this type of financial planning and anyone considering such a strategy must seek the help of a specialist accountant.

Do all really good accountants cost an 'arm and a leg'?

It depends on whether you look at it as an investment or an expense. Ask any really successful person and they'll always tell you, 'skimp on a lot of things, but never on professional advice'. Wise investors have great vision and they can see the advantages of investing in good advice. Most people just focus on the costs without looking at the benefits; if the immediate benefits outweigh the costs, then think of it as an investment.

It's extremely important for a successful investor to find a really good accountant. Do what the rich do and get the right people on your team. It's common sense. We all know that when you get the right players working together you win the game. It's a matter of getting the right people in the right seats, on the right bus, going in the right direction and doing the right things. You don't need to know everything there is to know about tax and property as long as you have a good accountant on your team.

> ❝ I reduced the tax she was paying on her rental income from $60,000 a year to $2,000 a year by transferring the properties... ❞

> **Another option is to fully gear all properties exposed to creditors.**

What are some of the different strategies available to investors for asset protection?

There are various strategies for asset protection that I suggest to my clients, each of these must be adapted to the individual's particular circumstances.

One option is to accumulate your assets in a separate entity, whether that is a trust, company or self-managed super fund. Let's look at trusts for a moment. There are different forms of trusts: discretionary trusts, unit trusts, hybrid trusts, blind trusts, bear trusts, testamentary trusts and the good-old super fund can also be a trust. Each has its pros and cons. For example, we don't recommend that our clients use discretionary trusts if the property is negatively geared because the losses are quarantined in the trust and you are unable to use them to offset the tax paid on any wages earned. In short, all properties should be held in a carefully planned trust structure because of the advantages associated with them.

Another option is to fully gear all properties exposed to creditors. By this I mean to borrow as much as possible on the properties so that there is very little equity in the property available to creditors. And finally, there are insurances that can be taken out to further minimise your risks.

What strategies can be used to pass assets on to family members?

If a property is passed on to a family member before the original owner dies, then CGT and stamp duty is payable, but there are no CGT or stamp duty issues if the property is passed on *after* the owner dies. The problem with this, as you can see, is that you have to die to avoid these tax issues. One way around this is to hold the properties in a trust, which allows the assets to be passed on with very little CGT or stamp duty (if any).

What are some of the ways people can hedge against the risk of losing their primary source of income and becoming unable to meet interest repayments?

As scary as it sounds, being unable to meet interest repayments is really not the end of the world. The bank will always work with you to find the best solution for both parties, rarely will they force you to sell your property.

If you have enough equity in the property, often the best solution is to 'capitalise' (or refinance) the portion of the interest that you cannot repay. It is preferable to capitalise the interest rather than to sell the property. Given that property doubles in value every seven to ten years, the extra amount owed in the form of the capitalised interest becomes negligible over time. Take for example a property valued at $600,000 with a loan owing of $250,000. If we cannot meet interest repayments and the bank agrees to capitalise interest, of say $50,000, the loan will increase to $300,000. When the property doubles to $1,200,000 the equity is now $900,000 ($1,200,000 less $300,000 loan) making the extra $50,000 owed almost insignificant. The best advice is to always hang onto your properties whenever you can.

Would you encourage people to invest overseas?

Personally, I have always preferred for my investments to be in Australia. I think there are enough opportunities within Australia to stay here and we have the benefit of a very stable government which creates the certainty that delivers predictable capital growth. When one goes overseas, one must contend with exchange rate fluctuations, lodging two sets of tax returns, having to keep abreast of many markets as well as banks being reluctant to lend to foreigners. Why do that when there is so much money to be made here without adding any more challenges?

What was your very first investment property and what did you have to do to get it?

Thankfully, I grew up with relatives who were all property investors, including my immediate family. As a child I could see the value in real estate doubling every seven to ten years. I didn't understand the science behind the increase at the time but could not dispute the fact that the values were increasing.

My opportunity came when I had just finished university and was three months into a new job. My father owned a property in Ryde (NSW) and decided he would sell it to me for $60,000. At the time it seemed unbelievably expensive and I didn't have the deposit, so Dad gave me a leg-up and loaned me the money. But he also made me treat the whole thing seriously, I took out my own loan and he kept the transaction at arm's length from himself. This lesson was the greatest gift he could have given me.

What is your personal property investment strategy and why do you take this approach?

In short, I follow a 'gearing' strategy rather than a 'savings' strategy. A savings strategy is simply too slow and won't allow an investor to take full advantage of a rising market. Gearing is about getting your asset base as wide as possible, as soon as possible, so that when the market increases your asset growth will compound much faster. When the value of each property increases, go back to the bank and borrow to the limit of what they will lend you. The more properties you have the more money you'll make, it's that simple. For example, if I have $1 million in property that goes up an average of 10% per year, then I will be earning $100,000 per year (while sleeping). Compare that to having only $500,000 in property which would earn me $50,000 per year at the same rate of growth. Which would you prefer?

What is the single most important lesson you've learnt about property investing?

Investing in property is not the same as trading property. The only thing that is the same about investing in property and trading in property is that they both use the same commodity, but the two activities are worlds apart.

When you *trade* property it is extremely risky because you are exposed to external factors that you have no control over, things such as the economy, interest rates, tourism, employment and world events all come into play. Trading is a business and it relies on skill and timing. When someone loses money by trading property it is really their lack of skill in timing that causes their downfall, not the market itself. The commodity they have chosen is immaterial; it could have been shares, scrap metal or even hamburgers! When you trade, it's about making a quick profit and you are relying on your skill and judgment to pick the market. It's a bit like gambling. Personally, I never, ever trade.

> **In another property I installed an air conditioner for $5,000 and got an extra $30 per week, that's a 31% return.**

Investing on the other hand, is not about making an instant profit. It's about buying and holding for the long term and never selling. Over time you will always make money. Think of it this way, property investing is completely risk free as long as you never sell. Because property doubles every seven to ten years, no one loses when they invest in the right property for the long term.

The stock market is completely different, even blue chip shares can disappear completely overnight, think about HIH, Ansett and One.Tel. Property will always be there.

If you had your time over again, what would you do differently?

First, I would have purchased more properties a lot sooner. I'd have had a long-term plan of buying one or two properties every year and stuck with that plan rigidly. Second, I wouldn't have sold any of my properties. It's always the same story, it felt right at the time but in hindsight it was the wrong thing to do. I've learnt never to sell.

When you have surplus cash, what are some of the ways you can add value to your property?

Every deal has the potential to achieve something extra. For example, I recently installed a carport in one of my rental properties for $3,000 and increased the rent by $25 per week, that's a 43% return on my $3,000. In another property I installed an air conditioner for $5,000 and got an extra $30 per week, that's a 31% return.

Apart from real estate, are there any other asset classes that you invest in?

No, nothing can show the same return with the same level of security.

In the future, what type of property will you invest in and why?

I will always go for median price residential property, where an average person on an average income would be the tenant. Median means the most popular price bracket in the area you choose. I will also stick to units and townhouses (as opposed to house and land) because the depreciation on them is much higher when compared with the same value house. The disadvantage is that typically you will have to sacrifice some of the capital gains you'd get with a house on separate title.

If anyone can succeed in property no matter what their current financial circumstances are, what do you think holds people back from becoming property millionaires?

In my experience, I have found that a number of factors hold people back. Some of the major ones are:

- A failure to take action – often people have the knowledge, but as we all know it's easier to do nothing.
- Fear of stepping out of their comfort zone – if you don't try anything new, you can never get hurt.
- Family and friends who impose their uninformed opinions on others, which leads to doubt and confusion.

If you had to start again with nothing, what would you do?

Exactly what I did before, which was to start my business at a young age when financial constraints were not so great and the risks of failure were not so critical. Make your mistakes at an early age, put your proceeds into property, continue to add to your property portfolio whenever the bank agrees to lend you more money, and wait.

What do you say to people who think it is too late for them to get into the market?

It's never too late.

What do you see as the major investment opportunities over the next ten to twenty years?

For some strange reason the property market has always started to move around the seventh year of the decade. The last property cycle started around 1997, ten years before that it was 1987 and ten years before that it was around 1977. So I don't expect any significant upward movements from the property market until 2007. While no one has a crystal ball, if you look at history you can reasonably estimate what might happen in the future. It's not an exact science but what is certain is that the property market has averaged around 10% growth per year over the last hundred-odd years.

The property market goes through cycles and when prices are flat it creates a lot of buying opportunities for those who are prepared to go against the pack. This takes a bit of courage, which can be gained from educating yourself; a depressed market is the perfect opportunity to buy more properties.

Who are the mentors that have inspired you, and what important lessons have you learnt from them?

My clients – some of them are truly inspiring. They never cease to amaze me with their knowledge and their ability to come up with creative ideas. From them I've observed the value in the tried and tested principle of never selling. The one insight that has been absolutely life changing for me is borrowing against the value of your property to fund your next investment and taking a portion of the borrowings to live off. This allows you to enjoy your life *today*, instead of waiting until you are 65. It also allows you to free-up the equity in your property without having to sell-down and reduce your asset base.

Most parents seem to be encouraging their children to go to university, study hard and get a high-paying job. Being a father yourself, do you think that's the best advice?

I believe that we all have to be realistic and work within our capabilities, as not everyone is a Michael Jordan in basketball or an Ian Thorpe in the pool. At the same time, although we all have the capacity to improve, we don't all have the desire combined with the entrepreneurial skills that will enable us to run successful businesses and make millions of dollars. My belief is that if you have average abilities and an above-average education, you will have a strong chance of earning a decent income and having a good lifestyle. But if you have average abilities and *no* education you will be destined to be poor. If my children have entrepreneurial abilities they will become successful people regardless of whether or not they are educated in the traditional sense. But there are no downsides to a good education and it certainly won't hurt them.

Another point I'd like to make here for parents is that what's really important is the *extra* education your children receive from you in matters of finance and wealth creation. I have already started my children's education about investing. That is the best thing I can do for them. It's not giving them material things, but rather the financial education that will allow them to acquire those things for themselves. Going through trials is what's called acquiring 'life experience'. Getting given something *without* going through the hard work of making the mistakes and overcoming the challenges is like passing an exam by cheating – you will

> **❝ Getting given something without going through the hard work is like passing an exam by cheating. ❞**

get the results on a piece of paper but you will not have learnt anything. It's in the doing that we receive the real value. It's about teaching a man to fish and not fishing for him, if you teach him to fish he can do it forever.

Are there any significant quotes that you live your life by?

I once read somewhere that, 'Success is 20% inspiration and 80% perspiration'. All the knowledge in the world won't help you unless you take action. Ultimately this is what differentiates the rich from the poor. There are no good or bad decisions, just consequences. We are the architects of our own lives. Where you are today is as a consequence of the decisions and actions you made in the past and where you will be in the future will be a consequence of the decisions and actions you take today.

THE POWER OF THE PAIR

Gary Leather
Jennifer Leather

GARY & JENNY LEATHER

> 66 Right now, we are building a development which consists of 132 units and eight townhouses...when it's complete it will be the largest solar-powered residential site in the southern hemisphere. 99

GARY & JENNY LEATHER

Gary and Jenny Leather were both born in 1958. They met and married while Gary was travelling in Australia, having left his home in Manchester, England, a few years earlier.

Not long after they were married, Gary started his first company, Leather Drafting, while Jenny was living her dream working as a children's hospital nurse. Over the years as the business grew Gary became disillusioned with the nine-to-five grind and Jenny's nursing wages were eroded by changes within the system. After more than two decades of working, they came to a point in their lives where they wanted more choices, more time to enjoy their family and a better lifestyle. It was out of this dissatisfaction that Jengar Investments was created – its objective was to create positive cash flow through property investing.

In its first eighteen months, Jengar Investments purchased 30 properties returning a positive cash flow in excess of $70,000 per year and creating equity of over $1 million. Jengar has dabbled in a variety of property investment strategies including, quick cash, renovation, vendor finance and rentals. Recently, Gary and Jenny began teaching personal development seminars to help other people along their journey.

The pair have been happily married for 22 years and have three teenage sons.

Why did you decide to start investing in property?

We both came to a point in our lives where we were thinking, 'There must be more to life than going to work five or six days a week. What can we do to buy back our time?' We both liked the idea of investing in property and had done quite well buying and building our own family homes.

[Jenny] As a child, I would often spend Sunday afternoons with my family looking at display homes and dreaming about what could be. Investing in property seemed an obvious direction for us – it was fun and something that we enjoyed doing together. It also gave us a common goal and purpose.

Through the books we were reading and the people we were associating with at the time, we decided to investigate the possibility of using positive cash flow properties, which would allow us to 'buy back our time' and give us the freedom we were looking for.

Were there any other types of investment or wealth creation opportunities that you considered?

We did investigate other wealth creation opportunities and what we learnt was that they didn't offer us the same benefits that property investment did. For example, with property *you* remain in control of the asset and when things change, they change slowly. With shares, things happen so much faster. To us the share market seemed quite volatile and for the most part we felt like we had no control. We actually got burnt in the dot-com boom (and bust) and lost a significant amount of money because we didn't know what we were doing.

[Jenny] I also looked at network marketing, but while that style of business has great mentorship and the opportunity to create passive income, the timing wasn't quite right.

> **To everyone's amazement, by the sixth month of that year, we had purchased eleven properties!**

It was only when we decided upon property as a common business interest that we began to experience remarkable success. The power of one plus one is eleven!

What is your personal property investment strategy and why do you take this approach?

Our specific strategy is to find and purchase positive cash flow properties – so the property must return more per month than it costs us to hold. Our strategy is magnified by looking for properties that are undervalued which allows us to get our investment back into our pocket as soon as possible, and move onto the next deal.

The reason we have chosen this strategy is so that the income from our properties will pay our own personal expenses, giving us greater time and freedom. By 'buying back time' we have a choice about what we do with our lives and can make the choice between *wanting* to work and *having* to work.

What was your very first investment property and what did you have to do to get it?

Our first investment was a small three-bedroom home in country Victoria, about one and a half hours' drive from Melbourne. Before we bought it, we researched the area and spent several days looking at properties. We put in lots of offers at around 20% below the asking price and were laughed at every time – you need a thick skin and have to be willing to make a bit of an idiot of yourself!

After we ran out of real estate agents in that town, we decided to call for help and contacted someone we knew who was already a skilled investor.

He guided us and gave us a more realistic view of the market. We were also very fortunate to come across a caring real estate agent who helped us to win our first deal at 10% below market price.

With very little property knowledge and no real experience, how did you acquire more than 30 properties in just eighteen months?

We both had a strong desire to get ahead, and so we decided to take money out of the equity in our own home in order to get things moving.

At a seminar that we attended, a stranger challenged us by asking if we had any goals written down. In 1999 we'd written the goal: 'It is now June 2006 and we are so happy and grateful that we are now in possession of ten positive cash flow properties'. He encouraged us to change the date and make it sooner. Even though we doubted that this would make a difference, we went home and changed the date, giving ourselves a crazy six months to purchase the ten properties. To everyone's amazement, by the sixth month of that year, we had purchased eleven properties!

[Gary] At that very same seminar, I had been chatting with a young investor who was involved in positive cash flow properties and at the end of the evening I asked this chap if he would be my mentor. Shortly thereafter, with the support of our new mentor, we were able to map out the initial steps involved in securing our first deal. We also made a joint decision not to spend any of the income that we earned through the property but to instead reinvest it back into the company to purchase more properties.

Our mindset was already positive because we had programmed ourselves for success before we even started; we had spent the previous two years listening to tapes, reading personal development literature and attending numerous seminars.

Was there a time when you thought it was all happening way too fast?

Yes, as a matter of fact there was one period of ten days in which we negotiated the purchase of seven properties – five in country Victoria and two in Tasmania. The fear of not being able to find the money made us cancel one deal.

[Jenny] Between the two of us, Gary has always had the belief that the money will be always be there, and guess what? He's right! My emotion went up because it was attached to fear – fear of failure and fear of losing it all. That's when I decided to take a step back and take some of the pressure off by using one of the 'out' clauses and cancelling the contract. Once the pressure had eased, I became calm, focused and my belief in myself returned. That's when everything proceeded smoothly.

What do you love about property?

We love meeting people from all walks of life and being able to talk and relate to them. We also love the fact that as a husband and wife team we have a common interest and can have lots of fun together. If someone had told us two years ago that we'd love getting up early, setting off to country Victoria and stopping off for a hot breakfast along the way, we would have thought they were mad because we loved our bed! Now we love going on adventures together, inspecting properties, doing deals, creating win-win scenarios and daydreaming about how we can add value to the properties we purchase.

It gives us enormous satisfaction when past and present tenants refer their friends to rent from us because we have been such great landlords. This tells us that we have developed a good reputation in town and it makes us feel really good about ourselves and what we are doing.

What do you think has helped you to get where you are today?

We are successful because we work so well together as a husband and wife team. Having a common goal and common purpose makes our relationship so much stronger. If either of us ever wanders off track, the other is always there to remind the 'wanderer' of our initial goal and focus. After all, we both want the same outcome in life.

[Jenny] It took us a while to understand and really appreciate our respective roles within the company. Gary is the dreamer and 'big vision' person and while this is definitely not my strength, I am able to take care of the detail. Together we have the whole picture covered, and are therefore able to put our plans into action.

If anyone can succeed in property no matter what their current financial circumstances are, what do you think holds people back from becoming property millionaires?

The word 'millionaire' and the fear of success often paralyse people. Most of us have been conditioned since childhood (by our parents, teachers, friends and other influential people in our lives) to believe that wealthy people are 'rip-off merchants', that they're greedy and take advantage of people. For example, your parents may have given you the feeling that wealthy people are unethical. And if this is the case you will have bad feelings about wealth and money. Because our past conditioning and thoughts control our present behaviours, we often get stuck and can't move toward a successful future.

A wise investor sees the desired outcome and his thoughts originate from that vision. Therefore his thoughts come from his future success and not from his past conditioning. We've learnt that it's imper-

> ❝ Together we have the whole picture covered, and are therefore able to put our plans into action. ❞

> **At around the same time the government changed the rules and my wages were halved overnight.**

ative that you are clear on your specific outcome because only then can your actions propel you in the direction of your desired results.

Are there any significant quotes that you live your life by?

Yes there is. It's this simple affirmation: 'Wealth, Success with Ease and Grace'. It might not seem like much, but think about the meaning behind each of the words and it can become quite powerful:

- *Wealth* – For us, wealth is not just about money. It's about relationships, family, career/business, health, lifestyle, service, education and spirituality. It's about all of the things that make up a complete, integrated and rich life.
- *Success* – You've probably heard the sayings that 'Success is a journey, not a destination' and 'Life doesn't happen in a day, it happens day-by-day'. It involves the steady progression toward one's desired goals and dreams, while at the same time having the commitment to persist through challenging times.
- *Grace* – This involves being able to recognise and appreciate your achievements along the way. It's also about gratitude and being thankful for what you do have rather than resentful of whatever you're lacking.
- *Ease* – Some people have the belief that in order to become successful you have to work really hard and sacrifice everything. That does not have to be the case. Generally, whatever you think about is going to create your reality. So if you decide from the beginning that things are going to be easy, then they will be.

Jenny, what made a nurse and mother of three decide to become a successful property investor?

While I loved my nursing, I realised that as I was getting older the job was becoming more physically demanding. At around the same time the government changed the rules and my wages were halved overnight. I became disillusioned with nursing and felt that I was certainly worth much more than I was being paid. Our children were that little bit older too and so much more independent. That's when I decided to look at other avenues to create choices for my family and for myself.

Gary was doing well in his business, but the more money he made, the more the taxman was taking away and I could see his frustration with the daily nine-to-five grind. We both realised that there had to be more to life than this.

Through reading books, attending seminars and speaking with people, we discovered that with property investment we could create structures that could protect our wealth. In addition, our expenses could be paid with pre-tax dollars. For example, if you buy a property at $100,000 with expenses of $5,000 and an annual income of $7,500, then the tax you pay is on the $2,500 (that is, the difference between the expenses and the income).

For us the benefits of being property investors far outweighed those of being wage earners. That's when we made our move.

What advice would you give to someone who wants to get started in property investing?

There's a whole raft of things that you need to know to be successful in property. But like most things, if you get the basics right the rest will eventually take care of itself. These are a few of the things that we've found to be important:

- *Know your outcome* – As Stephen Covey says in his book, 7 *Habits of Highly Effective People*, 'Always begin with the end in mind'. This means that you need to know exactly what you're aiming for, being as specific as possible.
- *Educate yourself* – You need to be committed to continuing your education, including improving your financial literacy. Ignorance may be bliss at the beginning, but very soon you may find that you have a

financial crisis on your hands! We've always believed in 'digging the well before you need it'. The more knowledge you acquire, the less likely you are to ever be in a position where your back is against the wall and you have to fight your way out.

- *Think abundance* – Realise that opportunities are always there. Don't live with a fear of lack, but rather have a mindset of abundance and always remain positive that you'll attract opportunities.
- *Be confident* – When you're starting out, sometimes you have to 'fake it 'til you make it', so don't be afraid to put on the appearance of being confident even though you may not feel like you are. If you do this for long enough, eventually you will become this person. So just keep going.
- *Focus on a strategy* – Once you know your desired outcome, focus on one thing – whether it is positive cash flow, property renovations, flips, vendor financing or so on. This helps to stop your mind from wondering and thinking 'now we've got the property, what do we do with it?' Make up your mind at the very beginning, stick to that decision and the universal power will give you what you desire.
- *Research thoroughly* – Do your due diligence to minimise risk. This includes understanding how much you can spend and how much you need to get back in rental income to put the property in the cash flow position you desire. For example, if you purchase a property at $100,000 you need to be looking at a return of $200 per week so that you are always net positive.
- *Listen* – Having great people skills means being a better listener than talker. This will allow you to negotiate a win-win outcome where both parties feel like they have done well. If you can't get a win-win outcome or feel like you're getting emotionally involved, be willing to walk away from the deal.
- *Calculate the risks* – A smart investor always looks at the worst-case scenario before going into a deal. This helps to keep your emotions in check. It is very important to control your emotions because often when your emotion goes up, your intelligence goes down and then you can't think logically or make good decisions.
- *Model others* – Learn to recognise the attributes in others who are already successful in the area that you want to be successful in and model them to improve those qualities within yourself.

How can a couple successfully work together in property?

First, the successful couple will commit to learning together. Unfortunately, when one party has a different vision to the other, it can negate both visions. For example, if one views life through lack and the other views life through abundance, then they are not acting congruently and without realising it, will sabotage each other's dreams. So if you're in a relationship and only one of you is planning to read this book, chances are down the track you will come unstuck. What we do is sit down and openly share our goals and dreams with each other so that we are both on the same page.

Second, make sure that you encourage each other and communicate frequently. For a couple to be successful in property, and happy for that matter, they need to build each other up, not pull the team apart.

From our experience, when we both became fully aligned with our goals, in an activity that we both enjoyed, then the 'power of two' became the 'power of eleven' and rewarding opportunities were soon attracted to us.

Jenny, in the beginning what did you come up against being a female investor?

I believe females tend to get a better deal from real estate agents. Perhaps it's because of our intuition and ability to chat. When you ask questions and show genuine interest, it is amazing what you can find out about the vendor's situation. Also, real estate agents (especially men) don't like to argue with a lady, so if you are a female investor you have a real advantage over the guys!

> " Make up your mind at the very beginning, stick to that decision and the universal power will give you what you desire. "

What are some of the lessons you've learnt about negotiating effectively to secure the best deal?

Show no emotion. Know your area. Know your rental property prices. Know the costs involved. Be willing to walk away. Remember, the highest energy wins and whoever is asking the questions is the one in control of the conversation.

Role play with your partner or friends or practise in front of the mirror until you become comfortable. It may seem a little quirky, but if you practise some of these skills and know how to project yourself in a negotiation it can save you tens of thousands of dollars.

What are some of your tips for successfully dealing with people?

Be a good listener and don't talk too much. Regardless of whether you are buying or selling, let the other person be the one to get excited and emotional.

If you need to build your confidence or speaking skills, join Toastmasters. This will help give you the confidence to express your arguments quickly and to effectively handle any objections that arise.

How do you develop the right mindset or mental attitude for property investing?

There are a number of things that you can do to develop the right mental attitude.

We started out by reading books. One of our favourites is Dale Carnegie's, *How to Win Friends and Influence People*. This taught us how to deal with people and improved our ability to negotiate. Another of our favourites is Napoleon Hill's classic, *Think and Grow Rich*. If you haven't read it, it's an absolute must.

Through our reading we became aware that it is our own ability to understand our minds that allows us to be in control. We have a personal philosophy that we call, 'T.F.A.R.'. This stands for: Thoughts, Feelings, Actions, Results. You see, what you think about affects the way that you feel, and the way you feel determines the way you act, and the sum total of all your actions ultimately determines the results in your life. Through this process, positive thoughts will give positive results and negative thoughts will return negative results. Only *you* can choose which thoughts you have because only *you* are in the driver's seat.

Sometimes in the beginning, in order to train your mind, you have to think deliberate thoughts to counteract some of the negative ones that are going through your head. These are called affirmations. There are a lot of books on the subject which can help you to learn how to think better quality thoughts so that you can ultimately achieve better results.

Another point is to have a big vision that extends beyond your own wants and needs. Our big vision may be to create wealth, but along the way we want to assist as many other people as we can which we do through our seminar teachings. Today, we also support a number of charities which really helps to get the focus away from ourselves and onto a greater cause.

We've also discovered that you need to be very precise about what you want and why you want it. Having a whole lot of 'airy-fairy' incompatible thoughts will only drain your mental power and you'll never be satisfied because you'll never know when you've reached your goal. What we say to people is take the time necessary to refine the dream. If your dream is to become a millionaire, why? Can you talk about it in detail or are you able to describe what it looks like?

Having said all this, the best thing to do is to simply ask yourself this question every single day, 'What am I doing and listening to today to increase my personal growth and financial awareness?'

> **Every time I walked past the picture, I would really feel the emotion of driving in that car.**

We all know how important it is to have goals. Is it just a matter of writing down a few things we want and then sticking them on the fridge?

Certainly that's one way of doing things and you're better off doing that than nothing at all. But we believe that you should give a lot more focused attention to your goals each day. You may have heard it said before – most people spend more time planning their annual holidays than they do planning their lives. How true that is.

We recommend that two or three times a day, you close your eyes and use the power of your imagination to visualise your goals for about ten minutes. Really put yourself in the picture; imagine how it will look, smell, sound, feel and taste. The more you engage your feelings and emotions, the more you are programming your subconscious mind to draw to you the things and people needed to materialise your goals in the real world.

It is also necessary to break your goals down into smaller objectives with achievable timeframes. By putting our goals into these incremental or 'baby steps', it allows us to better manage the goal and also stops us from feeling overwhelmed by one huge goal.

Gary, we hear that you're a big believer in creative visualisations. Can you give us an example of how it has worked for you?

I've always been a passionate believer in the power of creative visualisation. Some time ago, one of the things I wanted was a new Lexus. I found magazine photos of the car and made a collage which I would look at and daydream about the day I would drive it home. I wrote affirmations around this collage in bright coloured markers, which read:

I am in possession of this car by 30 June 2003. I am worthy. I am grateful. Believe – trust and it will happen.

Every time I walked past the picture, I would really *feel* the emotion of driving in that car. I'd close my eyes and visualise – smelling the leather and feeling the wind blowing through my hair. June 30 came and went, but I didn't give up the dream, I kept focused and would tell Jenny, 'It's on its way'.

Shortly after my birthday, Jenny bought me a Lexus key ring and we decided to take the whole family for a test drive. After the trip the boys acted as though the deal had already been done and it was already theirs! When I drove back to the lot, the dealer asked us how much we could afford to pay per month. I always thought we'd have to get a one-year-old car, but as it happened the car we were test-driving was a run-out model that had only done 55 kilometres and was classed as a second-hand vehicle. We negotiated a deal for that car for $10 less per month than I had originally written down in my goal and a few days later the car was ours (within three months of my goal date).

For some people, the fear of success is even greater than their fear of failure. Why is that?

It's funny, when you're young you believe you can do anything. One day it's a magician, the next day it's a Hollywood actor and the day after that it's a superhero. But as we journey through life, well-meaning people implant certain beliefs within us to protect us from getting hurt. They might say things such as 'Maybe you should think of a more realistic career', or, 'Just because you make a lot of money doesn't mean you are going to be happy'. It's said that in one's life there is a 1:10 ratio of positive-to-negative input.

All of this stuff builds up in our subconscious minds and from then on in, with every decision we make, we unconsciously match-up the new opportunity against those core beliefs – most of which were never ours in the first place. We then make a subconscious decision backed up by conscious logic, to either say yes or no and the sum total of all the things that we say 'yes' to ultimately determines where we end up.

So the question you need to ask yourself is, 'Are you happy with where you are at right now?' If the answer is 'no', then the reason is because you have certain beliefs around success that are working against you. What we suggest is that you draw a line in the sand right now and realise that you have the power to choose your thoughts. Remember, it is not what happens to us that is important, but rather how we choose to respond that makes all the difference.

How do people recognise what is holding them back and how do they move on from it?

There are a lot of different methodologies and processes for breaking through certain blockages within our own minds, including counselling, hypnosis, Neuro-Linguistic Programming, rebirthing, bio-energetics, the list goes on. However, on an individual level, it all comes down to managing your own 'self-talk'. That is, the words you say in your own head to yourself on a daily basis. If you go to any of Robert Kiyosaki's seminars, he'll often quote one of the sayings from the Bible, '...and then the word became flesh'. He says to be very careful about which words you use because words give power to your brain and will eventually bring about your reality. So if you say things like, 'I'm not good at numbers', or, 'I just don't have the confidence', or, 'I'm totally stressed out at the moment', then this is exactly what will continue. The more you say those things to yourself, the stronger they will become and the harder they will be to change.

We believe that what people need to do is to become more consciously aware of the things they are saying to themselves on a daily basis. A good idea is to carry a notebook with you and record your thoughts in it. Often when you see it on paper and read it back to yourself, you then realise how silly some of the things are and you can replace them with positive self-talk. To go one step further, you may want to wear an elastic band around your wrist and give yourself a flick every time you think a negative thought. People might think you're a little crazy, but after a while you start catching yourself before you think negative thoughts and replace them with something positive – thus creating a more productive neural pathway through the brain. Who would have thought a five-cent elastic band could help you to become a property millionaire!

How much time do you spend pursuing your property endeavours? And what are the key activities that you do?

[Jenny] I spend about twenty hours per week on our property endeavours. About ten hours per week is spent managing the administration and paperwork, namely tracking our properties, and the other ten hours is spent researching and looking for new deals on the internet. In addition to this, we both still consistently read motivational and personal development literature as well as attend seminars to ensure our continual self improvement. In other words, the learning never stops, the more you learn the more doors open.

Where do you see yourselves in the future?

Life is exciting at the moment. Over the last year we have formed a partnership with two other Victorian couples and together we are venturing into property development. It's great because we all bring different talents and skills to the project.

Right now, we are building a development which consists of 132 units and eight townhouses, with a combination of both lifestyle and sustainable living. We can boast, because when it's complete it will be the largest solar-powered residential site in the southern hemisphere, producing

> **Remember, it is not what happens to us that is important, but rather how we choose to respond that makes all the difference.**

Gary and Jenny's latest development.

80% of all its power needs. It'll also have an on-site 24-hour café and gymnasium, a lap pool and a 24-seat private cinema. We are very aware of water conservation and so have installed a state-of-the-art water recycling station and just recently we have been given a six-star energy rating.

For us this is only the beginning. Our goal is to build many more similar projects around the world, which will ultimately have a positive effect on the community, the environment and everyone who plays a part in the journey. Who knows, maybe one day we might even come across *you* on that journey? We wish you all the best, and remember, dream big and the universe will reward you.

RISKY BUSINESS

PETER COMBEN

> 66 When you get development approval and build your own investment property you truly buy at wholesale. 99

PETER COMBEN

Peter Comben was born in 1949 in Melbourne's eastern suburbs, where he has lived his entire life. He originally trained as a primary school teacher and spent sixteen years in the profession before leaving in 1986, having achieved the rank of assistant principal, to pursue his passion for property development.

His first property development was renovating a home he'd bought from a friend's parents. As fortune would have it, another friend walking past the home that Peter was renovating asked him if he could do a similar thing with a block of ten units he owned across the street. Peter agreed, and so launched his new career as a builder and property developer.

Peter soon realised his limitations though and teamed-up with a more experienced builder. Over the next seven years they completed many small to medium-sized residential developments as well as a number of major commercial projects. By 1997 Peter had returned his focus to units and small housing projects working with a team of sub-contractors.

The year 2000 delivered Peter one of life's 'aha' moments, with spectacular results. After attending a number of property investment seminars, he realised that he should be keeping rather than selling the properties he was developing. He now owns a significant portfolio of properties that he has developed or redeveloped himself. In 2002 Peter began presenting his own property development seminars based on his experience over the past twenty years.

Peter has been married for 25 years to Jocelyn who has now given up her job as a secondary school teacher to become his personal assistant – they have two grown up children.

How did you become involved in property development?

I've been a full-time property developer for the past sixteen years, prior to that I was a primary school teacher and had worked my way up to the position of assistant principal. While I enjoyed teaching, I couldn't see much in the future other than more of the same for the next 25 years. I was in a comfort zone and had grown accustomed to the security that a salary provides. So, I took leave without pay to try something different and never went back to that salaried teaching job.

My parents invested in property when I was young and I always enjoyed helping Dad renovate their properties. Believe it or not, the first thing I bought when I turned eighteen was not a car, but a block of land. Having that experience early in my life sparked an interest that I took advantage of as I became older.

When I left teaching I started a home improvement business; I built pergolas and timber decks, and landscaped gardens. In doing this work for other people, I began to see that I should be doing it for myself. I took an opportunity that came along when a friend's parents were selling their house to move to a retirement village. I bought their home, renovated it, and sold it for a profit.

It's interesting that even though you might not do that well out of your first project, it often sets you up for the next one. While I was working on this house, a friend walking his dog admired what I was doing. It turned out that he owned ten units on one title, on the other side of the street. He employed me to renovate the units and I soon realised that there was more potential in the project than renovating in the way he wanted. He simply wanted to get his money out of the property and put it into something else. I suggested that he should put the units on separate titles and sell them one by one. It turned out that by separating the titles we increased the value of the project by 30%.

> *...a house in Launceston, Tasmania, sold for $171,000 with a weekly rental income of $465.*

I learnt a valuable lesson from this project. It is what I call the 'multiplier effect'; we renovated ten units instead of one property and ended up with ten profits. From then on I was determined to build and develop multiple units so that I could multiply my profits. But I had a common problem, a shortage of cash flow. Rather than go back to teaching, I became a registered builder. I soon realised my limitations and in 1989 formed a company with an experienced builder. During the next seven years our company completed many small to medium-sized residential developments as well as some commercial projects. However, my creativity was being restricted because I was spending so much time administering the growing company. And besides that, I was building for other people and not for myself. That's when I got serious about doing my own developments.

What exactly is property development?

There are different ways of defining 'property development'. My definition, in simple terms, is any alteration or change to a property that increases its value.

There are several ways to develop property. The most basic form of property development is renovating. The renovation could be as simple as painting the front door or replacing the carpets; it is amazing how simple things can create perceived value in a property.

The next step up from a renovation is extension. This could include anything from adding on an extra room out the back, to creating a second storey. Be cautious before attempting this strategy and don't assume that an extension will make you money. Many people make the mistake of extending a property beyond its value – that is, the increased value does not cover the cost of the extension. The last thing you want is an overcapitalised house with little land value. When you do your numbers it may be better to demolish the house and build a new one.

Another way of extending a house is to construct an additional dwelling in the backyard. For example, a house in Launceston, Tasmania, sold for $171,000 with a weekly rental income of $465. This very large positive cash flow came from the additional three bungalows in the backyard, which produced significant rental income in addition to the house.

By far the most powerful way of developing a property, I believe, is subdivision. If you are going to get involved in property development, this is the strategy that you should really understand. Put simply, subdivision is creating smaller parcels from a larger piece – whether it is land, units or a high-rise development, subdivision involves the creation of many titles from the original single title. With subdivision, we see property development at its most extreme and its most profitable.

What does a property developer do?

A property developer is the person who conducts an orchestra of property professionals. The developer co-ordinates everything from sourcing the deal, organising the finance, putting plans together, getting the development approval, overseeing construction, to finally selling the completed project. The entrepreneurial developer does not necessarily do the work him or herself, but manages a team of experts to do the work for them.

Why would someone consider becoming a property developer?

If you are already a seasoned property investor, chances are you could apply a lot of your property knowledge to becoming a good developer. A very large part of being successful in development is the ability to do your research and to be accurate with your numbers. As a property investor, you already know what it takes to make sound investment decisions; property development requires similar thorough homework. Having creative abilities and being entrepreneurial also helps.

Although property development is more challenging than straight investing, it is also more profitable. And development provides an outlet for creativity, which you otherwise don't get from standard investing. Speaking from experience, driving past your developments, that were once just ideas or 'concepts', is very satisfying.

What do you think are the essential qualities of a successful property developer?

I once thought that I needed to be a builder to be a good developer. While it has helped me to have structural knowledge and a greater understanding of the building process, a true developer does not need to be a builder. You don't necessarily have to be the one out there with a nail gun and power saw.

The most important personal attributes of a developer, I believe, are good communication and management skills. Much of the work of a developer is building and managing a team. Creativity is also important, you need to be able to visualise the development 'concept' before any ground is broken. You need to be decisive and able to take action quickly. To make a rapid decision you need to have done your due diligence and research so that you know your market and can identify a good deal when it comes along. Organisational skills and multi-tasking are also vital; you need to be able to manage a number of people and tasks at one time. In addition, you need to be discerning about where to focus and on which deals to spend most of your time. Another quality is the ability to remain highly motivated. It's one thing to say, 'I want to be a developer and create profits, positive cash flow or capital growth investment properties', but it's another thing to remain motivated when a deal falls through or you have trouble with a planning application or the construction of a project.

Above all, don't be greedy. Many developers come unstuck because of greed. Never compromise good ethics for the sake of making money. In the property industry, word travels fast and your name sticks. As a developer, your reputation is critical – it is your lifeline to future opportunities.

What are some of the different types of developments you have done?

Perhaps the best way to teach you about property development is to run through one of my more recent projects.

An agent told me about a family living in Vermont, Victoria, who wanted to sell their backyard. They had this funny little weatherboard house at the front and wanted to create a 'battleaxe' block behind. Battleaxe blocks have a long driveway down the side of a house with a sizeable piece of land at the back; in my opinion, these don't make the best development sites.

The agent organised a meeting with the owners and I found out that the reason they wanted to sell their backyard was because they had six children and needed the money to pay for an extension to their little weatherboard house. I had a look around and came up with a better solution. I said to them, 'Instead of selling the backyard, how about we look at a 'Plan B', whereby you could have your ultimate dream home, the home you'd perhaps never thought possible'. I could see their eyes light up. 'How about I pay for and build you a two-storey home at the back of the block while you continue to live in your existing house,' I said, ' and when it's complete, you can move straight in and we'll knock down the old house and build three new units at the front'.

To make it really come alive, I showed them photos and later that week took them through a similar house I'd built.

> **66** As a developer, your reputation is critical – it is your lifeline to future opportunities. **99**

They could touch it, feel it and imagine themselves living in it. Guess who loved it? The wife, of course!

One of the things I continually emphasise to people is the importance of creating win-win deals. The win for them was that they would end up with a very large two-storey home on land that was big enough for two units. Another thing they said was really important to them was their fibreglass pool, which their kids absolutely loved and couldn't be without. I wanted them to be happy so I agreed that we would move the pool into their new backyard. Often it is minor things like a fibreglass pool that will make a deal happen. I let them alter the layout of the house in any way they chose, which didn't matter a whole lot to me but it made a big difference to them. So, they ended up with their six bedrooms (how many houses have six bedrooms these days?), they got their pool and were able to continue living in the same location, with the same neighbours and the kids going to the same school.

Peter's Vermont development 'Under Construction'.

The only other challenge we had to deal with was getting our equipment into the back half of the block. I negotiated with the neighbour to obtain access, which allowed the family to stay in their old house while the new one was being built. All the neighbour wanted was a small payment by way of me paying for a new side fence.

Construction went ahead and the family went on with their lives. They didn't have to put a cent into the project or think about the hassles of construction. It was great to see the kids come down and watch excitedly as their new home was being built. Once it was complete, they moved in and we demolished their old house. We could then get moving with the three new units, from which our profits in the project would be derived.

All this made the project take twice as long to complete, but when you see the numbers, you'll know it was worth it. The cost to me in building their house and a few other incidentals was about $300,000. What did I get back for the $300,000? I got the land for the three units for free. Total costs for the project included $440,000 for the construction of the three units plus $300,000 for the family home, totalling $740,000. I sold one of the units for $340,000, I kept one valued at $360,000 and another valued at $380,000, totalling over $1 million. So the net profit was a cool $340,000 (effectively, the value of one unit).

What are some of the risks associated with property development and how can they be managed?

As with any type of investment strategy, you need to sufficiently manage the risks in such a way as to ensure that they don't turn into headaches. These are a few risks unique to property development that you need to pay close attention to.

Council delay – If you make a deal to buy a property conditional on gaining development approval (in return for payment of a small option fee to the vendor) and there is a delay in gaining approval, there is a risk that your option will expire. The easiest way to hedge against this risk is

> **There is the risk that you may not get the approval you want, or indeed any approval at all.**

to make sure that you have an option with a longer time period than you think you will need. For example, if you think approval will take six months, negotiate an option for twelve months. Alternatively, you could include an extension clause in the option contract that will allow you to extend the length of the option in exchange for an additional amount to be paid to the owner.

Can't get approval – There is the risk that you may not get the approval you want, or indeed any approval at all. To manage this risk, make sure you do your due diligence thoroughly before going into the project. I encourage people to seek the advice of a professional who knows the planning provisions of the locality, inside-out. You can't be entirely certain you'll get the approval you want, but provided you have secured the site with an option, you can always choose not to exercise that option and walk away from the project. You will have lost considerable time and money getting the project to that stage, so you cannot entirely eliminate this risk.

Can't sell the approval – If you are doing a pre-packaged development (which I'll discuss later), there is the risk that at the time of selling you won't find a buyer for the development. This usually occurs because you haven't done a proper concept evaluation before you started.

Financial risk – There may be additional expenses that you have not identified which cause your costs to blow-out. Make sure that you do a detailed feasibility study from the beginning. Check and re-check your figures and get them looked over by a more experienced developer.

Building risk – Once you have planning approval, and you know that you will make a profit, you still have risks associated with building. For a lender, construction loans are one of the highest risk loans that can be made. Some knowledge of building is helpful to keep an eye on the construction process. Do your due diligence on the builder you are going to use for the project. Inspect their workmanship on previous developments so that you know what the end product will look like and make sure you have regular site meetings with your builder. Pay your builder on time – you don't want him walking off the job because he hasn't been paid.

Building delay – Manage this risk through your building contract. Pay the builder a fair price if he delivers on time and put in place penalties or ways of getting out of the contract should the project run over time.

Market risk – You don't want to build what the market doesn't want. Oversupply can be the biggest killer and can eat up a significant chunk of your profit. Studying the demographics, knowing what other developments are happening in the area and talking to local real estate agents to get a feel for what buyers are looking for can help to prevent this.

Understand that there are downsides, there is no doubt that property development is a risky business. You need to put in the time, mental effort and research. You need to have courage and patience. But believe me, the hourly rate is second to none.

Can you explain the strategy of selling an approved development site?

As a developer, you have the option of putting together what I call a prepackaged development and on-selling it to an investor or builder – this allows you to get the 'first harvest' out of the project without having to worry about the hassles of building.

Let's go through some of the key elements of pre-packaged developments.

First, you need to find an appropriate site. But before you can find a site you need to know what you are looking for. Ask yourself questions such as where you want the development to be? Why you want to develop in that location? What a perfect development would look like in that locality? What development is going to suit that market? As you get involved in developing, you tend to work a particular area. You get to know the good streets, the bad streets and the places people like to live. You develop what I call 'developer's eyes'. That is, you are able to see the land's potential, rather than what is on the land at the moment. You also need to study the relevant local planning code so that when it comes to driving around looking at property, you already know what block size and zoning you are seeking.

Once you have found a site, you need to formulate a development concept for it. If you are not familiar with the planning codes you should seek the advice of a planning expert such as a town planner or a good architect. It is important to know what you can and cannot build on the site before you start making offers to buy it.

You need to do a detailed feasibility study of the project to see how much profit can be expected. If you are going to secure the project there is a lot of work ahead and you want to make sure you'll be handsomely rewarded for it. Remember that any potential lender will want to see a fair profit (say 20% of development costs) before they will finance it. The more profitable the deal, the easier it is to get finance.

It is only after completing these steps that you should think about making an offer. I would suggest that you negotiate a way to hold the site while seeking development approval. You want to find a way of taking the property off the market, while still having the option to pull out of the transaction if you can't get the approval you want. The most common way to secure a development site is to use an option, which gives you the right but not the obligation to buy the property at a certain price within a predetermined period of time. Alternatively, you may want to consider a joint venture with the owner of the property (as I did with the family with six kids). Make sure you have a solicitor on your team by the time you get to submitting offers or writing option agreements.

You are now ready to seek development approval from the local council. For this, I suggest that you have some experienced professionals on your team. Don't try to save money and do it yourself. In property development, the money you spend on your consultants will come back to you tenfold.

Some of the consultants you will need at this stage include someone who is familiar with the local and state planning provisions, a draftsman or architect to do your drawings, a surveyor, and depending on the complexity of your project, a stormwater/drainage expert, traffic engineer and there may be others as well.

When you have gained approval for the development, you have the choice of taking the 'first harvest' from it and selling it as a pre-packaged development or continuing to build. If you decide to sell, you need to find a buyer. To whom would you be selling this project? There are many people that are builder/developers who will complete the project. They will make their builder's margin, plus a bit more. When you're putting together a pre-packaged development, you have to factor in a generous profit for the next person to complete the project. You can't take the full profit otherwise no one will buy the project from you and you won't make any friends. The typical time it would take to do such a pre-packaged development in today's market would be between six and twelve months, depending on the efficiency of your team and the local council.

Computer generated impression of a future project.

> *...when you get development approval and build your own investment property you truly buy at wholesale.*

This strategy is very profitable. The idea of pre-packaging a development is not something that is novel or unique. There are many people in Australia and around the world who are doing this day-in, day-out. They make a more than generous income every year just by finding sites, securing them through options, getting approvals and on-selling. I know people who have become specialists in this and are making millions of dollars every year. However, if you do have the capital and know-how to see a project through to completion, that's when you really see your profits compound.

Why do you now build most of your projects rather than sell them?

The alternative to selling the site with development approval is to build the development yourself. This is now my core business. Obviously, there is more money to be made by selling five nicely-finished townhouses to five different purchasers than selling one bit of dirt with a permit to a builder.

In the past, I chose to complete my developments to produce extra cash flow. I would buy into a development, complete it, sell it and then move on to the next. This made us a lot of money, but we also had to pay a lot of tax.

A few years ago, I attended a number of investment seminars. I was listening to these guys talking about acquiring investment properties and how to get discounts. That's when I had one of those 'aha' experiences. I thought to myself, 'Wow, I've already got the vehicle'. I realised that I should have been keeping many of the properties I had developed rather than selling them. The greatest lesson I have learnt about property is this: as a developer you can build your own investment properties at wholesale prices. There is a lot of talk about the word 'wholesale' these days, but when you get development approval and build your own investment property you *truly* buy at wholesale.

If you need the cash, it's fine to sell. But if you are looking to invest, what better vehicle is there than development? You have the potential to build your investment portfolio at a considerable discount to the average investor. Just imagine – if you build five units with a profit margin of 20% cent each, you'll get one for free!

How do you source finance for your projects?

Sourcing finance for a development project is a different ball-game to sourcing funds for a simple residential investment. Your ability to source finance for a development will depend on the profitability of the project rather than your ability to service the loan. There has to be a profit margin otherwise finance will not be forthcoming.

The golden rule for financing development projects is to use other people's money (or the bank's money). This can be daunting for first-time developers. When faced with a project with a low profit margin, the rookie developer will often finance the project from his or her own funds. This is a mistake. If banks won't lend money for a development project, chances are that it is not a good project. Don't try to finance the project with your own funds just because you can't get finance. You end up taking all the risk. It may be the case that you need to hold the property for a number of years until the market moves sufficiently for you to be able to prove the profit in the project before you obtain finance to build.

Does GST affect developers?

Those three horrible letters! Yes, the GST *does* affect developers, whether in a multi-unit development or a subdivision. You need to ensure that you keep accurate records and that the GST is in the feasibility study when calculating your profit.

The GST can be very confusing for developers and it is even more complicated when you are an investor who wants to invest in your own development. So it's best to check with your accountant.

What are your top tips for becoming a successful property developer?

1. Have realistic goals about what you want to accomplish. It is far better to build wealth slowly and keep it, than to build it too fast and lose it overnight.
2. Always maintain your integrity and focus on building strong relationships with *everyone* you meet. In the same way as you will want to see a builder's history of projects, an investor or joint venture partner will want to see yours.
3. Find a good personal mentor who has vast experience in development and a genuine desire to see you succeed. When you find such a person, be willing to accept their feedback, sometimes it is a mentor's job to tell you what you don't want to hear. The more knowledge of the development process you can acquire, the better you manage your risks.
4. Focus on gathering the best possible team around you. This will take time and effort, but it is well worth it. If you find the right people to have on your team, the time taken to get approval and to work through issues will be reduced and you will be able to get your projects completed quicker, so the profit will be greater. I've also discovered that it's one thing to build a team, but it's another thing to keep the team together. Always look at creative ways to reward the people you work with.
5. Do the numbers, do the numbers, do the numbers. You need to know the benefits for each party involved and the exact profit before you begin. You also need to be crystal clear about what you are looking for, which will help you to quickly and accurately identify development opportunities.
6. When building your own projects, retain as many of the properties as you can. As a developer you have the privilege of being able to build

your portfolio at genuine wholesale prices. Think long term rather than getting excited about making a 'quick buck'.
7. Property development is not for everyone. Don't think it is a way to cut corners and get to the top quickly. Too many people go into development starry-eyed and get washed up twelve months later. It is a risky business with more than its fair share of challenges, so think long term, think win-win and stay in the race because the rewards are certainly worth it.

How would someone learn more about property development?

Unfortunately, there are not a lot of books on property development. There are a handful of property development workshops and I have recently put together one of my own. Here are some of the things that I cover, which is perhaps useful as a guide to what you should look for in a property development seminar:

- How to source properties with development potential. As most are not advertised, you need to learn how to source the right property. Remember, profits are made at the start of the project.

- How to do win-win joint ventures with property owners to leverage off the owner's equity in the project.
- How to assess a project in view of the various planning issues.
- How the development approval process works, how to consult with councils and how professionals can help you.
- How to conduct a financial feasibility assessment.
- What you need to know about project financing (without finance there is no deal).
- What you can do to manage risk.
- How to get the best builder and how to get the project looking right.
- How to find the right professionals to work with.
- The correct way to sell your properties off the plan.
- How to build up a property investment portfolio through development.

Make sure you find out how property development works and understand all elements of the process. If you acquire this knowledge, you will much more successfully manage the risks involved in property development. You can imagine that for me, a school teacher going out into the world of property development, I didn't know much. I had to ask questions, lots of questions. If you can't find a solution to a problem, it means that you haven't found the right person to ask.

Are there any significant quotes that you live your life by?

I have many, but if I had to choose one, and relate it to property it would be, 'Do unto others as you would have them do unto you'. At the end of the day, property is a *people* business. Every day we speak with agents, vendors, tradespeople, consultants, tenants, neighbours, banks, investors and the list goes on. You need to be aware of the interests of others. You need to be able to consider a deal from the other person's perspective. Work hard on improving and maintaining good relationships with people.

FREE BONUS GIFT

Peter Comben has kindly offered a FREE BONUS GIFT valued at $19.95 to all readers of this book...

Property Development Checklist – This checklist was compiled to assist people who want to break into the development game. It takes you step-by-step through exactly what you need to do – from sourcing the site, to council approval, to finding a builder – right through to selling or leasing your development. It is an absolute must for anyone ready to make big profits.

Simply visit the website below and follow the directions to download direct to your Notebook or PC.

www.SecretsExposed.com.au/property_millionaires

FINAL THOUGHTS

We trust that you have enjoyed reading this book as much as we've enjoyed putting it together. As you can see from these successful property investors, there are many different paths you can take on your road to financial freedom. What is refreshing is that despite their differing approaches, most of their ideas have a consistent theme:

1. Start now! Many have the knowledge, but few take action. Remember that the opportunities are everywhere, all you need to do is get out there and find them.
2. Set some clear and specific goals by beginning with the end in mind. It is also important to map out a purpose-built plan for how you are going to achieve those goals.
3. Actively look for mentors; experienced investors that have already built a substantial property portfolio and can offer you sound advice.
4. When you discover an opportunity, make sure that you do thorough due diligence. Nearly every investor agreed that you make your money when you buy.
5. Remember that property is a 'people' business. That's why it's important to build a good team around you and to treat people with a high level of integrity and respect.
6. Understand that duplication is the key. In other words, one property doesn't make you rich, but many will. So always think about how you will finance the next deal.
7. Finally, realise that we can never know all there is to know about property. As your wealth grows, make sure that you continue to set aside time for self-development and acquiring further knowledge.

From where we sit as the collaborators of this book, the passion and enthusiasm that these people have for property investing is evident. Creating a well-structured property portfolio is certainly an exciting journey and one that is absolutely worth the time and effort.

We hope that this book has been of great value to you and we truly wish you the best of luck for your future.

Dale Beaumont and Colin B. Fragar

P.S. We love receiving letters or emails from people who have been inspired by something shared in one of our books, so please contact us with your tales of inspiration.

Email: info@SecretsExposed.com.au

Mail:

Dream Express Publishing
PO Box 567
Crows Nest NSW 1585
Australia

P.P.S. Ten per cent of the profits from this book will be donated to Mission Australia, an organisation which aims to empower disadvantaged and isolated individuals, families and communities by giving them the support they need to get back on track, and lead more fulfilling lives. It also offers housing support initiatives for homeless people and those at risk of homelessness. For more information or to donate directly, please visit www.mission.com.au.

How To Claim Your FREE Bonus Gifts Valued Over $147

Some of our contributors have generously offered FREE bonus gifts for all of our readers. Here are some of the things you'll receive simply by visiting our website:

FREE GIFT # 1 ($35.00 Value) 47 Tips and Tricks for Property Success – In this fun and extremely informative eBook, Craig Turnbull shares 47 tips and tricks compiled during his twenty-year property career. Jam-packed with useful ideas, this eBook will save you thousands of dollars and fast-track your path to financial freedom.

FREE GIFT # 2 ($22.95 Value) 11 Power-Packed Strategies For Negotiating – Over the last few years, leading buyers' agent Patrick Bright has purchased over $300 million worth of real estate for his many clients. In this special report you'll learn eleven tried and tested strategies for negotiating the best deal every time. Apply just one of these strategies successfully and you can save tens of thousands of dollars on your next property purchase.

FREE GIFT # 3 ($49.00 Value) How To Climb The Money Tree – Hans Jakobi, Australia's Wealth Coach® and best-selling author, has already helped thousands of people achieve financial independence. In this special eBook, Hans will show you how to attract more money, riches and happiness into your life. Plus, he will reveal the ten must-know steps to becoming a millionaire in today's market.

FREE GIFT # 4 ($25.00 Value) 7 Rules of Renovating for BIG Profits – In this special report, you'll learn how to renovate a property quickly, easily and cheaply, and sell it for top dollar…or use the equity to fund your next deal. Plus, you'll learn the 8 Deadliest Renovation Mistakes most people make, and how to avoid them.

FREE GIFT # 5 ($19.95 Value) – Property Development Checklist – This checklist was compiled to assist people who want to break into the development game. It takes you step-by-step through exactly what you need to do – from sourcing the site, to council approval, to finding a builder – right through to selling or leasing your development. It is an absolute must for anyone ready to make big profits.

Simply visit our website and follow the directions to download your free gifts:

www.SecretsExposed.com.au/property_millionaires

* The FREE bonus gifts offered by contributors are current at the time of printing. If a particular gift is no longer available, we will substitute another gift of similar value and content. For the most up-to-date information please visit: www.SecretsExposed.com.au/property_millionaires

** The intellectual property rights (including trademarks and copyrights) associated with each of the bonus gifts offered are those of the respective creators. Unauthorised distribution, modification or copying of any of these documents is prohibited without the express written permission of the creators.

About the Authors

Dale Beaumont

Dale Beaumont was born in Sydney in June 1981. Growing up, he participated in a number of sports and at the age of nine was selected for the elite NSW Gymnastics Squad. Training 34 hours per week, he soon learnt the value of discipline, hard work, having a coach and most importantly, delayed gratification.

After six years of intensive training, Dale changed his sporting focus to competitive aerobics so that he could spend more time on his studies and pursue other interests. In 1998 he became the National Aerobics Champion and the youngest Australian to compete at the World Aerobics Championships, where he placed eighth.

After finishing high school, Dale began attending various personal development and success seminars, where he learnt from people such as Jim Rohn, Michael Rowland, Bob Proctor, Robert Kiyosaki, John Maxwell, Brandon Bays, Brad Sugars, Mark Victor Hanson and many others.

At the age of 19, together with good friend Brent Williams, Dale wrote his first book titled *The World at Your Feet,* and co-founded Tomorrow's Youth International, which now runs educational and self-development programs for 13 to 21-year-olds in four countries. Dale has been featured on the *Today* show, *Sunrise, Mornings with Kerri-Anne*, as well as in countless newspapers and magazines.

Most recently, Dale has been hard at work developing the 'Secrets Exposed' series, to bring together the very best material from hundreds of Australasia's most successful people. With more than twenty books planned for the next three years and an up-coming seminar series, Dale is now a sought-after speaker on topics such as; Up-start Business, Networking Skills, Book Publishing, Internet Marketing and Generating Publicity.

Dale lives in Sydney with his beautiful and very supportive wife, Katherine. With a baby next on the 'to-do' list and lots of international travel plans, Dale is looking forward to the challenges ahead, and to spending more time enjoying life.

For more information about Dale's workshops and educational materials, or to book him as a guest speaker at your next conference or event, please visit: **www.DaleBeaumont.com**

Colin B. Fragar

Colin B. Fragar was born in the Blue Mountains of NSW, in 1982. After finishing high school, he took a part-time job and began studying a combined law and business degree at the University of Technology in Sydney.

At the age of nineteen, Colin purchased his first investment property. It was a small cottage which he renovated with the help of family and friends. After increasing the value of the cottage by more than 40% in six months, Colin developed a passion for property and began reading as much as he could about the subject. After purchasing a second property, he started doing small sub-divisions and developments. Still at university, Colin was awarded an international scholarship to study finance in New York where he met some amazing people and expanded his vision of what could be accomplished. Upon his return, he sold one of his properties he purchased six months earlier, the profit more than covering his university exchange expenses.

Colin recently graduated, having topped several of his subjects. He has decided against taking up offers to work in law, choosing instead to build and expand his own property development company. At last check, and at just 23 years of age, Colin's property portfolio was valued at $1.7 million. However, with more of his time now freed up, his goal is to at least double that in the next eighteen-months and to one day own his own CBD building.

Despite his success Colin humbly believes that it is his integrity and passion for life that are his most valuable assets. He also attributes much of his success to the team of colleagues around him, as well as to the support of family and close friends. When he's not working, you'll find Colin sitting thoughtfully on a cliff edge in the Blue Mountains or at Church helping others. His ultimate goal is to become financially successful so that he can better assist those in need.

For more information about Colin's property success and development projects, please visit: **www.ColinBFragar.com**

About Our Contributors

We would again like to say a huge 'thank you' to the people who have helped to make this book possible. Some of our contributors have their own books and other educational products – for more information, contact them directly.

Craig Turnbull
Address: PO Box 225 Leederville WA 6903
Phone: 1300 132 941   Fax: 1300 136 843
Email: info@iaspire.com.au   Website: **www.iAspire.com.au**
Books: *It's Easy to Invest in Property*, *It's Easy to be a Property Millionaire*, and *Unlimited Cashflow – It's Easy to Make Money in Property*

Patrick Bright
Address: PO Box 311 Neutral Bay NSW 2089
Phone: 1300 732 724
Email: patrick@patrickbright.com   Website: **www.PatrickBright.com**
Books: *The Insider's Guide to Buying Real Estate* and *The Insider's Guide to Profitable Property Investing*

Dymphna Boholt
Address: PO Box 944 Buderim Qld 4556
Phone: 1300 850 944   Fax: (07) 5450 0834
Email: admin@dymphnaboholt.com
Websites: **www.DymphnaBoholt.com** or **www.WildlyWealthyWomen.com**

John Fitzgerald
Address: Custodian House 7027 Nerang-Southport Road Nerang Qld 4211
Phone: (07) 5527 4999   Fax: (07) 5527 4955
Email: info@jlf.com.au   Website: **www.UntoldWealth.com.au**
Books: *Seven Steps to Wealth* and *We Can be Heroes*

Gordon Green
Address: PO Box 2221 Milton QLD 4064
Phone: 1800 776 348   Fax: (07) 3510 5444
Email: info@pbccentre.com   Website: **www.pbccentre.com**

Hans Jakobi
Address: PO Box 167 Portland NSW 2847
Phone: (02) 6355 5800   Fax: (02) 6355 5855
Email: support@realestateinfo.com.au   Website: **www.RealEstateInfo.com.au**
Books: *How to Be Rich and Happy on Your Income*, *Financial Freedom…Starting Now*, and *Due Diligence Made Simple*

Rick Otton
Address: 139/272 Victoria Avenue Chatswood NSW 2067
Phone: 1800 003 588   Fax: (02) 9475 4367
Email: info@rickotton.com   Website: **www.RickOtton.com**

Sam Vannutini
Address: PO Box 281 Bentleigh VIC 3204
Phone: (03) 9557 3255   Fax: (03) 9557 3255
Email: info@renovateforprofit.com   Website: **www.RenovateForProfit.com**
Books: *Renovate for Profit*

Ed Chan
Address: Suite 5, 55 Grandview Street Pymble NSW 2073
Phone: (02) 9391 5000   Fax: (02) 9391 5050
Email: reception@chan-naylor.com.au   Website: **www.Chan-Naylor.com.au**
Books: *How to Legally Reduce Your Tax*

Gary & Jenny Leather
Email: leathers@bigpond.net.au

Peter Comben
Address: PO Box 686 Brentford Square VIC 3131
Phone: (03) 9893 4757   Fax: (03) 9893 4757
Email: info@smartpropertydevelopment.com.au
Website: **www.SmartPropertyDevelopment.com**

Other great titles now available

Secrets of Male Entrepreneurs Exposed!

In this book you'll discover...

- How to come up with your multi-million dollar idea
- Creative ways to raise hundreds of thousands in capital
- How to build and lead a champion team
- Unique marketing ideas that will explode your profits
- Master techniques to influence people and sell your ideas
- What it takes to get media exposure and loads of free advertising
- How to package and franchise your business to go global

Featuring written material by...

Jim Penman (Jim's Mowing) • **Siimon Reynolds** (Photon Group) • **Justin Herald** (Attitude Clothing & Intimidate) • **Phillip Mills** (Les Mills International) • **Tom Potter** (Eagle Boys Pizza) • **Brad Sugars** (Action International) • **Tim Pethick** (nudie Founder) • **Douglas Foo** (Apex-Pal International) • **Michael Twelftree** (Two Hands Wines) • **Domenic Carosa** (destra Corporation) • **Jim Zavos** (EzyDVD) • **Craig Lovett** (Cleanevent International) • **Glenn Kiddell** (VitaMan Skincare) • **Trevor Choy** (Choy Lawyers) • **Carmelo Zampaglione** (Zamro) • **Andrew Ward** (3 Minute Angels)

Secrets of Female Entrepreneurs Exposed!

In this book you'll discover...

- The skills of starting and running your own business
- How to establish your client base and deliver a professional service
- The secrets of networking and creating business partnerships
- Creative tips for finding and training your team
- How to receive media publicity and lots of free advertising
- What you need to do to expand your business ideas around the world
- How to effectively balance business success and family life

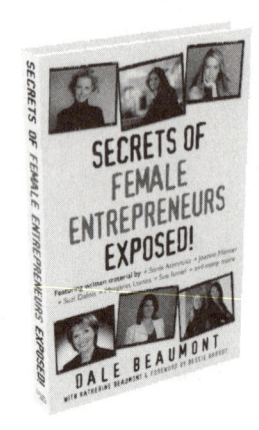

Featuring written material by...

Sonia Amoroso (Cat Media) • **Joanne Mercer** (Joanne Mercer Footwear) • **Sue Ismiel** (Nad's Hair Removal) • **Carol Comer** (High Impact Marketing) • **Sue Whyte** (Intimo Lingerie) • **Kristina Noble & Simone Babic** (Citrus Internet) • **Sandy Forster** (Wildly Wealthy Women) • **Katrina Allen** (DeJour) • **Suzi Dafnis** (Pow Wow Events) • **Tanya Bension** (Corporate Training Australia) • **Amy Lyden** (Bow Wow Meow) • **Margaret Lomas** (Destiny Group) • **Suzy Yates** (Baystreet Mediaworks) • **Kristina Karlsson** (kikki.K) • **Shelley Barrett** (ModelCo.) • **Kirsty Dunphey** (M&M Harcourts)

To order your copies online and SAVE, visi

...or coming soon

Secrets of Young Achievers Exposed!

In this book you'll discover...

- What it takes to become a real success
- How to know what you want to do with your life
- How to get motivated and stay motivated
- How to overcome criticism and discouragement
- What all super-achievers have in common
- How to reach the top of any career, *fast*
- How to turn your dream into reality

Featuring written material by...

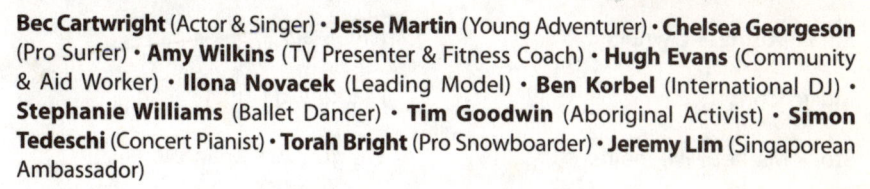

Bec Cartwright (Actor & Singer) • **Jesse Martin** (Young Adventurer) • **Chelsea Georgeson** (Pro Surfer) • **Amy Wilkins** (TV Presenter & Fitness Coach) • **Hugh Evans** (Community & Aid Worker) • **Ilona Novacek** (Leading Model) • **Ben Korbel** (International DJ) • **Stephanie Williams** (Ballet Dancer) • **Tim Goodwin** (Aboriginal Activist) • **Simon Tedeschi** (Concert Pianist) • **Torah Bright** (Pro Snowboarder) • **Jeremy Lim** (Singaporean Ambassador)

Secrets of Great Public Speakers Exposed!

In this book you'll discover...

- Why the ability to communicate in public is critical to career success
- What all successful speakers have in common
- How to overcome fear and project confidence to your audience
- How to plan and structure a presentation for maximum impact
- How to use the right type of humour and have your audience in stitches
- Simple techniques to communicate subconscious messages
- What it takes to make $1 million a year as a professional speaker

Featuring written material by...

Doug Malouf (Speaking Coach) • **Shelley Taylor-Smith** (World Champion Athlete) • **Carl Barron** (Leading Comedian) • **Matt Church** (Top Corporate Speaker) • **Catherine DeVrye** (Best-selling Author) • **Billy Graham** (Boxing Champion) • **Gavin Blakley** (Former Toastmasters President) • **Ron Tacchi** (Founder of Speaker Seeker) • **Wayne Berry** (Australasia's Leading Sales Trainer) • **Robyn Henderson** (Networking Expert) • **Ron Lee** (The Corporate Ninja) • **Peter Sheahan** (Youth Speaker) • **Candy Tymson** (Gender Differences Expert) • **Michael Rowland** (Personal Development Speaker) • **Amanda Gore** (Aussie Speaker in USA) • **Chris Rewell** (Image Consultant)

www.SecretsExposed.com.au

Contributors Wanted For Future 'Secrets Exposed' Books

Yes, you can now be involved in the creation of a number of other exciting titles in the 'Secrets Exposed' series, including:

High Achievers	Inspiring Leaders
Film Actors	Great CEOs
Sales Professionals	Sporting Heroes
Small Business Owners	NRL Stars
Music Icons	Marketing Gurus
Stock Market Millionaires	Weight Loss Champions
AFL Stars	Aussie Exporters
Big Business Tycoons	Personal Development Coaches
Great Team Builders	Soccer Stars
Profound Parents	Winning Franchises
Aussie Sporting Legends	Powerful Women
Amazing Innovators	PLUS MANY MORE…

You can help to share the secrets of Australia's most successful people by nominating a contributor, and you'll be credited in the 'acknowledgements' page of that book!

To nominate a contributor for any of the above works, or to suggest another 'Secrets Exposed' title, please send your ideas in writing to:

Dream Express Publishing
PO Box 567
Crows Nest NSW 1585
Australia
Email: info@SecretsExposed.com.au

Discover The Amazing Success Behind Australia's Leading Educational and 'Life-Skills' Program for Teenagers and Young Adults

After five years and more than 7,300 thrilled participants in four countries, your teenager NOW has the opportunity to experience the highly acclaimed 2½ day advanced life-skills seminar *'Empower U'* . . .

- Do you feel that your teenager could be achieving more, but can't seem to get them motivated?
- Do you want to give them the *best* education possible?
- Do you want them to have every means at their disposal to live a happy, successful and rewarding life?

Then you need to discover WHY thousands of parents agree that the 2½ day *'Empower U'* program is the best decision you can make for your son or daughter's future…

In a fun, teenager-friendly environment, Dale Beaumont and Brent Williams will reveal the very same motivation and high-achievement secrets that propel the world's top performers to success – and that are already working wonders for thousands of kids across Australia. Secrets that your child will learn and apply to their life immediately. Secrets we've made so simple to understand and use that you will notice *immediate improvements*.

At *Empower U* your child will become so motivated, so focused, and so determined to succeed that they could well become a super-achiever in a very short time. Your child will walk away from *Empower U* with total *belief* in their own abilities and absolute *certainty* that they can achieve anything they want. Plus, they will have a 'toolkit' full of specific strategies they can use to convert their desires into tangible, real-world results - starting right away!

It doesn't matter whether your child just needs some friendly encouragement or a total 'attitude overhaul', *Empower U* will give them the belief, tools and strategies they need to get moving in the right direction.

"I am so glad that a friend told me about Empower U. My daughter attended almost two years ago at the age of fourteen. She is now seventeen and more motivated than ever. I think the most amazing thing about her experience is that it was not just a one-off. They have supported her the whole way and that has been just terrific."

Peter Stacey   (Father of Jessica)

"My two daughters attended the Empower U program. One excited, one sceptical. The change in both of them is truly amazing. I am now such a big fan and I just hope that more people take the chance on this that I did. Because then they will see what I now see."

Tura Lechminka   (Mother of Alana and Kathryn)

Whether it's more motivation, improved attitude, better exam marks, a savings plan, landing a great job, or just a more open family relationship … you will see results *FAST!*

To enrol your son or daughter into the next *Empower U* program simply give us a call or check out our website…

Tomorrow's Youth International

1300 732 782

www.TomorrowsYouth.com.au